The University of Glasgow:
1451–1996

The University of Glasgow: 1451–1996

A. L. Brown and Michael Moss

Edinburgh University Press
for
the University of Glasgow

© A. L. Brown and Michael Moss 1996
Edinburgh University Press
22 George Square
Edinburgh EH8 9LF

Designed and typeset in Janson by Fionna Robson, Edinburgh
Origination by Baynefield Cartographic, Edinburgh
Printed in Scotland by Bath Press Colourbooks

CIP Data for this book is available from the British Library

ISBN 0 7486 0871 0 (hardback)
ISBN 0 7486 0872 9 (paperback)

Contents

Acknowledgements

The authors are grateful to Dr John Durkan and Dr James Kirk, Dr Robert Thomson, and Profesors Archie Duncan, John Gillespie, John Gunn, Arthur Kennedy, Robert Rankin and Tony Slaven for their contributions and comments on the text, and to Trevor Graham, Manager of the Photographic Unit, for his patience and assistance.

Permission to print photographs has been generously given by Alan Blackburn of Roshven (pp. 30–1), the Royal Faculty of Procurators (pp. 33–5), Mr W.A.C Smith (p. 41), *The Herald* Newspaper (pp. 45, 80 and 113), the Scottish Record Office (p. 67 upper) and Professor J. Willock (p.98).

CHAPTER 1

The College on the High Street, 1451–1870

Glasgow University was founded by Pope Nicholas V in a letter dated at St Peter's in Rome on 7 January 1451 and authenticated with a lead papal seal or 'bull'. It erected a 'studium generale' or university for all future time in Glasgow – in theology, canon and civil law, in arts and in all lawful faculties with all the privileges, liberties, honours, exemptions and immunities enjoyed by the 'studium' at Bologna and it is still the authority by which the University confers degrees. It tells that it was issued at the request of King James II of Scotland, but the initiative probably came from the bishop of Glasgow, William Turnbull. He had been born in the Glasgow diocese at Bedrule near Jedburgh, studied at the University of St Andrews and in several continental universities, became a leading minister of King James and for some time his agent at the papal court. Turnbull must have believed that a university would enhance the status of his Cathedral and diocese and provide educated clergy for the western parts of Scotland, the area from

which most of its students came until very recent times. Turnbull's career and his university were not unique. Scots had for some time been travelling to universities abroad and three other early universities were founded in Scotland – St Andrews in 1413 and Aberdeen in 1495 by papal bulls; Edinburgh with royal approval by the town council in 1583. Scotland was relatively small and poor but not isolated, and it already had a strong interest in education. England, for example, had two larger collegiate universities, Oxford and Cambridge, from the thirteenth century but no other until the 1820s. The Scottish universities were small but until two generations ago a higher proportion of Scots, and Scots from a wider range of society, came to them. Scotland had and still has a distinct and more popular tradition in education.

Turnbull's university was a small college in a small town of perhaps two thousand inhabitants. Glasgow had developed long before as a market centre beside the lowest ford on the

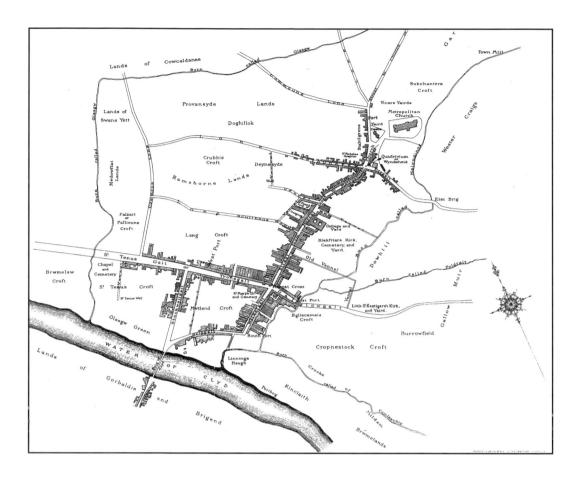

Glasgow in the mid-sixteenth century.

River Clyde and by 1286 a bridge had been built slightly down river where the Victoria Bridge now stands at the foot of the 'Briggait' – the Bridge Gate. The modern street names and street plan still show the outline of the medieval trading town built mainly of timber. From the thirteenth century it expanded slowly north, up the High Street hill, towards a second centre round the Cathedral where, according to tradition, about the year 600 a holy man, St Kentigern or Mungo, established a church and a monastery on the site of a graveyard consecrated two centuries earlier by St Ninian,

the first Christian missionary to Scotland. The coats of arms of the University and the city still display objects associated with Kentigern's miracles. This tradition determined that the new or restored bishopric in Strathclyde was in Glasgow and from about 1114 there was a stone Cathedral on the old site at the head of the High Street. The walls of this Cathedral and its successor in the 1190s were rediscovered recently below the floor of the nave of the large, mainly thirteenth-century Cathedral which still stands there to-day. An engraving made by John Slezer in the 1660s shows the Cathedral, the bishop's castle and the canons' square, stone houses in the Cathedral precinct. A few hundred yards south are the new seventeenth-century buildings of the University and beside it the church of the medieval Dominican priory – Blackfriars. In the background, down the High Street hill, is the merchant city by the river with its houses and steeples. The Cathedral and the University are set in a green and largely open area and, though many of the buildings in the engraving are later, the area at the head of the hill must have looked much the same in 1451. The city began to change radically only in the eighteenth century when trade with the Americas and the beginnings of industry led to a rapid increase in population to over 70,000 by 1800, over 300,000 by 1850 and over 750,000 by 1900. It expanded far beyond the old centre and the buildings of the University, still mainly those in the Slezer engraving, were by the 1840s in an over-crowded, run-down area polluted by industry. The old site

was sold and in 1870 the University moved to new buildings on a green site two miles west, at Gilmorehill beside the River Kelvin. The land to the north and west were soon built over but the River Kelvin preserved an open view across the city to the south and Kelvingrove Park protected it to the east, and almost all the university departments with sixteen thousand students are still on Gilmorehill. It is ironic that grime from domestic chimneys and heavy industry on the Clyde gradually darkened the 1870 buildings and that industrial decline since 1915 is allowing the rain slowly to clean them. Salmon are again running up the Kelvin, literally within yards of the University.

Slezer's view of Glasgow in the late seventeenth century.

In 1451 the new university had no property and little funding but it was soon alive. The bull of foundation was probably read first to the Cathedral clergy and we know that it was publicly proclaimed on Trinity Sunday, 20 June, at the Cross at the foot of the High Street. The first recorded university meetings and the first lecture in July were in Blackfriars and over fifty students including a number of clergy from the Cathedral and religious houses in the diocese had enrolled when teaching began in October. University meetings were in Blackfriars and in a chapel or one of the two chapter houses in the Cathedral, and living and teaching accommodation was rented, probably in a modest building later called the Auld Pedagogy on Rottenrow (Rat Row) near the Cathedral. Bishop Turnbull died in 1454 and, though he had obtained privileges such as freedom from taxes for his university, he had not been able to endow it. A sizeable building on the east side of the High Street, immediately north of Blackfriars, was however rented from James, Lord Hamilton. In January 1460, for the honour of God, the most blessed Virgin Mary, St Kentigern and all the saints, and for the souls of himself, his wife and his relatives, Hamilton granted the entire property to the principal regent, the senior teacher, in the Faculty of Arts and his successors as a College, asking in return only daily prayers and services for himself and his family. This was the turning point for this 'old, strong, plain building', as an English traveller described it in 1636, with a number of chambers and small rooms around two courtyards with a long strip of land behind it as far as the Molendinar Burn and four acres beyond it on Dow Hill; this remained the site of the

University until 1870. The Hamilton building was replaced on the same ground plan but on a much grander scale in the mid-seventeenth century and further buildings were added in the eighteenth and early nineteenth centuries. By good fortune and generosity the University had become securely housed on a prime site fronting the High Street with land on which to expand.

Some universities had several colleges but Glasgow had only the Hamilton College, and College and University became almost synonymous terms. During its first century the University may at times have had over a hundred students, but often there were no more than sixty, sometimes even fewer. The bull of 1451 authorised the creation of all faculties but most students studied Arts and only small numbers sought higher degrees in theology and canon or civil law. Arts students normally entered as boys, some as young as ten, with a grounding in Latin, the language of teaching and, at least officially, of conversation in the University until the eighteenth century. They could obtain their 'licence to teach', the Bachelor of Arts degree, in three years and become Masters of Arts after a further year but many did not graduate. In 1451 printing was only on the point of invention and teaching consisted largely of dictating a text, commenting on it and having the students dispute (debate) matters it raised. This was appropriate in a course which consisted primarily of philosophy, mental and physical, largely based on the works of the ancients, in particular of Aristotle. It began with logic and rhetoric, proceeded to mathematics, arithmetic and geometry, to the physical sciences such as

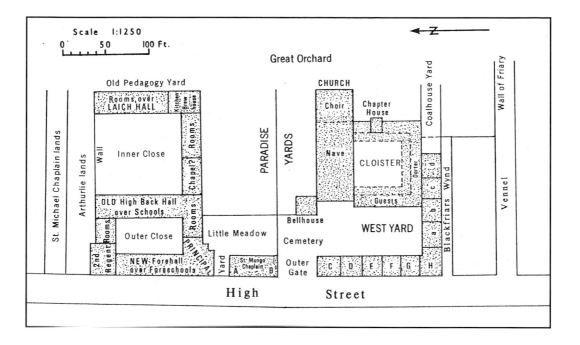

Scale 1:1250

0′ 50 100 Ft.

Great Orchard

Old Pedagogy Yard

Rooms over LAICH HALL

Inner Close

OLD High Back Hall over Schools

Outer Close

Little Meadow

NEW Forehall over Faraschools

PARADISE YARDS

CHURCH

Choir

Chapter House

Nave

CLOISTER

Guests

Bellhouse

Cemetery

WEST YARD

Coalhouse Yard

Wall of Friary

Blackfriars Wynd

Vennel

St. Michael Chaplain lands

Arthurlie lands

Outer Gate

St. Mungo Chaplain A B

C D E F G H

High Street

Plan of the medieval College and Blackfriars (on the right).

astronomy and optics, and to ethics. The same teacher, called a regent, took his students through the whole course. Students were examined by oral questioning for as long as the sand ran in a timing-glass. They lived in the College under the tight discipline of their teachers during a university year which at first lasted from mid-October until early September with only brief holidays – though with many 'holy days' without classes. The quality of student life depended on ability to pay. Poorer students shared rooms and beds. At the two meals, mid-day and evening, wealthy students ate well with the regents and paid accordingly while poorer students might act as servitors and had to be content with 'short commons'. They rose at five in the summer, six in the winter, and spent much of the morning and part of the afternoon in class. There were regular prayers and services and on Sundays and great feast days the students proceeded in a 'troop', a crocodile,

to the Cathedral for Mass and were counted in and out by the regents! There was much ceremony and formality at all stages of university life. There were games – archery and football were popular and it may have been a football injury which obliged Robert Ross in 1476 to seek a papal dispensation to be ordained despite being blinded in one eye when struck by a cabbage stalk while playing with another student!

The University was closely associated with the Cathedral and governed by what, even now, seem very comprehensive statutes and regulations. Its most senior officer, the chancellor, was the bishop, from 1492 the archbishop, of Glasgow, though he rarely took an active role. The chancellor is still its most senior officer – since 1858 elected by

The fifteenth-century silver-gilt University mace.

the graduates. The rector was the head, the presiding officer, of the University; he headed processions, summoned and presided over meetings of masters which alone could make university statutes and over his council. He was invariably a cleric, often a canon or official of the Cathedral, appointed by agreement among the seniors though nominally chosen by the four 'nations', the constituencies to which all teachers and students were allocated according to their place of birth – originally Clydesdale, Teviotdale, Albany and Rothesay, areas of Scotland with Ireland included in Rothesay. Nations, with different boundaries, were abolished only in 1977 and the students still elect a rector every three years. The teachers were the regents, those who 'ruled' the schools, and it was in the early eighteenth century that professors teaching a defined subject finally replaced them. The 'principal' regent of normally three regents had charge of the building, the College, and from the late sixteenth century he became the Principal, the head of the University, as he is today.

The buildings and the manner and content of teaching changed over the centuries but there has been a strong, continuous strand since 1451 through the great changes of the Reformation, the expanded scholarship of the seventeenth and eighteenth centuries and University Reform in the nineteenth century. In a sense the greatest changes have taken place since 1945 and even these have not entirely destroyed the old traditions. The University Mace is a symbol of this continuity. From 1451 there were several maces carried on formal occasions and processions but soon collectors were appointed to raise funds for a specially fine mace and in the 1460s a silver mace, 'the crown partly gilt and ornamented with blue enamel', was purchased, probably from Germany. It has been in use ever since save for thirty years after 1560, the year of the Scottish Reformation, when the chancellor, Archbishop James Beaton, fled to Paris taking with him some of the archives and valuables of the Cathedral and the University, including the university mace given to him by the rector for safe-keeping. The archives never returned and were destroyed during the French Revolution but the mace was sent back in 1590. It is still carried on most formal occasions and it was only in 1971 that a second, simpler, mace was given to the University for other occasions in commemoration of James Watt (page 20).

The weakness of the medieval and early modern University was inadequate funding. Payments and gifts were required from students, but most were given directly to the teachers and officials to supplement the income they received from church offices. Most students were at least in minor holy orders and preparing for a career in the Church though by the early sixteenth century some laymen, the sons of gentlemen and burgesses, were attending classes. Some of the teachers were notable men, in particular John Major, principal regent from 1518 to 1523, one of the last great scholastic philosophers and theologians, an international scholar, who wrote *A History of Greater Britain*, both England and Scotland, published

Slezer's view of the Old College and Blackfriars in the late seventeenth century.

in 1521. The lowest period in the history of the University came in the years before and after 1560, the year of the Reformation in Scotland. Student numbers fell and for a short time there may have been only one active teacher. The reformed Church however placed particular importance on education from parish school to university, and the following twenty years saw better funding and, literally, the renewal of the University.

The First Book of Discipline, a blue-print for the reformed country prepared in 1560 by six leading Protestant reformers including John Knox, in its plans for universities ordained that Glasgow should have two colleges, one for arts, one for philosophy, civil law, Hebrew and divinity, and forty-eight bursars. This never materialised but benefits did follow. A letter of Mary Queen of Scots dated at Glasgow in 1563 says that only one part of the school and chambers of the University was in repair and the rest, both dwellings and provision for poor bursars and masters to teach, had 'ceissit' and she gave the manse and the 'kirkroom' of the confiscated Glasgow Blackfriars with thirteen acres of its land and some of its revenues to the University to support five poor bursars. In 1573 the town council of Glasgow, which in 1567 had received a grant from the Queen of all the city's chaplainries, altarages and prebends and the possessions of the Black and Grey Friars to maintain ministers and provide hospitals, agreed that, because these were now adequately funded, the properties should be redirected to the University. At the annual Commemoration of Benefactors the University still remembers the care bestowed by the City 'upon the preservation of the University in

times of civil warfare and commotion'. There were other grants, almost always of church revenues, often disputed and slow and difficult to collect, but a major part of the University's income until the early nineteenth century.

What was now needed was a scholar and a strong personality to take advantage of the new spirit and 'renew' the University. The General Assembly of the Kirk, at the instigation of James Boyd, the first Protestant archbishop of Glasgow and chancellor of the University, and the rector, Andrew Hay, a former canon of the Cathedral and now a local minister, provided the man when they invited Andrew Melville, recently returned from Geneva, to become principal regent. He accepted and though he remained only from 1574 until 1580, he oversaw the renewal of the University. He was a St Andrews graduate who had studied in Paris and Poitiers, taught in Poitiers and in John Calvin's city of Geneva - where he studied theology with the celebrated Protestant scholar Theodore Beza. When he came to Glasgow he had the assistance of only one regent and he did much of the teaching himself. By the time he left he had three regents and, instead of taking a group of students through the whole course, they specialised in their teaching – they 'professed' subjects.

The manner and order of teaching was not wholly new but there were major changes and new subjects. The emphasis was on the liberal arts and on useful knowledge to be found particularly in the wisdom of the ancient world. The provision for Greek and Hebrew, necessary for Biblical study, was also made more stable. The quality of teaching attracted more students and renewal culminated in 1577 in a remarkable royal charter which reflects the spirit of the time and Melville's own ideas. It begins 'Since Divine providence has brought us (King James VI) to the government of the kingdom, in these times in which it ordained the light of the gospel to illumine our country of Scotland, and the darkness of popery to be dispelled, and it behoves us to be specially concerned that so great a blessing of God should be transmitted to our posterity, and since by no other means can that be so conveniently done as by a sound education and right training of youth in learning which will soon wholly perish unless it be fostered by honours and rewards'. It then grants the College 'pining in poverty' the rich parsonage and vicarage of Govan, three miles away on the south side of the river, to support the principal, his servant, three regents, a steward, four poor students, a cook and a janitor. It confirmed all previous grants and re-erected and re-founded the College. The keystone of this re-foundation or Nova Erectio, which largely determined the method of government of the University until 1858, was the Principal to whom the whole College was made subject – though with prudent provision to correct him if he was careless or erred! He must teach Divinity and therefore be well versed in Holy Writ and skilled in languages, in particular Hebrew and Syriac. He was to lecture for at least an hour each day, alternately on the Scriptures and on their languages. On Saturday he was freed to prepare his Sunday discourse in the church of Govan. When a vacancy occurred the chancellor archbishop, the rector, the dean of Faculty and five local ministers were to elect the new Principal within a defined time-table. There

were to be three regents and in their first year students were to be taught rhetoric and instructed in Greek to prepare them to study philosophy. Dialectic, logic and moral philosophy followed; in the third year mathematics, arithmetic and geometry; and in the fourth, the observation of nature, geography, astronomy, general chronology and the computation of time from the creation of the world a form of history. Regents were to be the most learned preceptors that could be found to train the young men in teaching, writing, declaiming, debating, with the utmost diligence in the field of letters. And there was much else in the charter. Some changes did not last– even the old system of unspecialised regenting was restored in 1642 and continued until 1727– but the quality of teaching was now better and the University never looked back. Melville's nephew wrote, with pardonable exaggeration, that there was 'na place in Europe comparable to Glasgow for guid letters, during these yeirs, for a plentifull and guid chepe mercat of all kynd of langages, artes and sciences'.

The medieval University had been primarily a college for churchmen and the reformed University remained the same until the late seventeenth century. Indeed the influence of the Church remained strong at least throughout the nineteenth century. Before 1560 the University had relied heavily on the clergy of the Cathedral and the diocese; after 1560 it depended as much on the ministers of the west of Scotland. The regents were for long almost all ministers and the Principal was required to be a minister until 1858. The first lay Principal was indeed Sir Donald MacAlister in 1907. The majority of the 100–150 students in the College in the

seventeenth century intended to proceed from Arts to Divinity and become ministers though not necessarily to graduate in either. It was only in the eighteenth century, as student numbers increased steadily to over a thousand by 1800, that the proportion of divines dropped sharply and even attendance at Sunday service in the College became thin.

The finances of the University were stronger after 1577 but ecclesiastical revenues, confiscated endowments of cathedrals or abbeys and a share in the revenue of parish churches were precarious and in danger of confiscation by the Crown, and, if reports and accounts are to be believed, the University had to struggle to meet even ordinary costs. It is therefore remarkable that in the late 1620s it had the confidence to embark on a project to replace all the buildings and almost to achieve this within thirty years. Even more remarkable, this was done during a time of intense political and religious controversy and civil war. King James VI had disputed with the reformed church in Scotland, and in particular with Andrew Melville, about royal authority. In 1603 James became also King James I of England and he and his successors, rarely in Scotland, were often at odds with their subjects in both countries over civil government and over the governance and faith of the church. The latter touched matters of immediate concern to members of the 'reformed' College. Some left it because they could not conform to religious change and some fought in the civil wars. The University itself navigated the storms remarkably well. The new buildings were begun

The imposing West Front of the Old College.

when Charles I, James' son, was disputing with his subjects in both kingdoms; carried forward during the great Civil War, King Charles' execution and during eleven years of interregnum including the Protectorate of Oliver Cromwell; and completed as Charles II was restored in 1660.

The need to replace the fifteenth-century Hamilton buildings had been apparent for many years. The two courts or closes, west nearest the High Street and east nearest the gardens, were inadequate for the number of students; parts were dilapidated; and the thatched and slated roofs needed frequent repair. A bold decision was taken to rebuild on the same site and plan, and work began at the end of 1631. On the first day thirty-four carts of stone were delivered; nine men were employed in the east court and they, the carters and the barrowmen were bought ale at a cost of over £20 Scots to celebrate the event. Building continued in stages as money was raised and by 1660 the two courts were virtually complete and the decorated west front facing the High Street was in place. The buildings round the new courts were grander, more regular, more solid than the old. Most had rooms on three levels, the uppermost at roof level, with large dormer windows. It resembled an old Oxford or Cambridge College and it would have been familiar in any European university city. Entry from the High Street was through a wicket in the large studded wooden doors in the centre of the decorated and gilded west front. Part of this is rebuilt at Gilmorehill as Pearce Lodge but gives no impression of the solid mass of the High Street frontage. Immediately inside the gate was a handsome

series of arches or piazza and ahead, astride the arched passage to the east court, there was a tall tower with a bell to regulate classes and for which a clock was ordered in 1686. The east court was larger with six external tower staircases giving access to the floors. There were rooms for teaching, many chambers for teachers and students, a common (dining) hall and the usual domestic offices. Richer students could have the luxury of decorated chambers; poor students crowded into garrets and truckle beds. These buildings, considered to be the finest of the period in Scotland, are well recorded because most survived until the move in 1870 to Gilmorehill where the original buildings have many echoes of the 'Old College' (page 47).

The most remarkable feature of the seventeenth-century buildings is their funding. The University had virtually no capital of its own and in 1630 Principal Strang opened a subscription list 'for the building of a commoun librarie within the colledge of Glasgow furnishing thairof with books and utherways inlarging the fabrick of the said colledge to the publick and privat use of the students'. In the event the Library gained little but the appeal brought a remarkable response. The first entry in the book of donations is a grant of £200 sterling (£2,400 Scots) on 14 July 1633 by Charles I on his visit to Scotland to be crowned. Beneath is the note – 'This soume was payed by (Oliver Cromwell) the Lord Protector anno 1654' – five years after Charles's execution. The second entry is a promise of a thousand merks Scots by the Marquis of Hamilton,

The Gatehouse of the Old College.

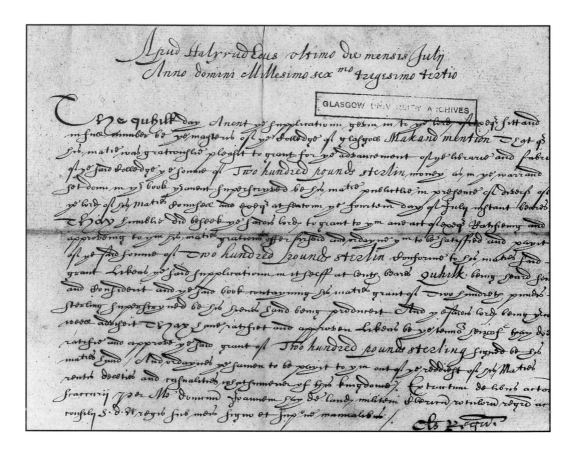

Promissory note from Charles I to provide £200 sterling endorsed as paid by Cromwell.

who was executed two months after King Charles, but honoured in 1656 from his estate. These apart, between 1630 and 1637 over 40,000 merks Scots* were given or promised by fifteen Scottish noblemen, many lords and lairds, nine Scottish bishops, and very many ministers of the kirk, by towns collectively and townsmen individually, and by Scottish courtiers and merchants in London. The majority of donors came from west and south-west Scotland. The archbishop of St Andrews and two successive archbishops of Glasgow each gave a thousand merks.

The provost, baillies and the council of Glasgow gave more than two thousand merks. The Earl of Stirling gave £500 Scots to build one or two chambers 'bearing my name and armes for the use of my children and such of my house as sall have their breeding therein in all tyme coming' but to be used at other times as the College thought fit. And there were many smaller donations. It reflects a striking belief in education and in the College in Glasgow.

As building progressed there were crises when funds ran out and delays because of political uncertainty. Money was borrowed – the regents themselves were lenders. The

* A mark or merk in Scotland was two-thirds of a pound and at this time an English pound was worth twelve pounds Scots.

14

minister of Glasgow, Zachary Boyd, a Glasgow graduate who held university offices over a long period, bequeathed a large sum with the provision that two chambers should be at the disposition of him 'whoo is the chiefe man of the name of Boyd' and his generosity was marked by his bust set in a niche above the archway between the two quadrangles. By 1640 the east and north sides of the east quadrangle were built and by the early 1650s, with the help of Boyd's money, the entire quadrangle was complete. By 1660 the west quadrangle and the Principal's house were built. The panel over the entrance from the High Street bears the date 1658 and a royal coat of arms was hastily purchased to place above it when Charles II was restored to the throne in 1660. Further additions were made later, notably in the 1690s the Lion and Unicorn staircase in the west quadrangle which is now at Gilmorehill. The University had a fine new home funded by the generosity of a large number of well-wishers and supporters.

Life in the new buildings changed slowly. In mid-century the 150 or so students, most of them boys in their early teens, assembled at six on weekdays, seven on Sundays, attended prayers twice a day and the kirk twice on Sunday. The regents were responsible for their spiritual welfare and every student was required to have his own bible and read it. They must wear red gowns inside and outside the College and speak only in Latin. In 1642 'lawful games such as gouffe, archarie and the like' were held to be licit but carding and dicing were forbidden. These at least were the rules. Classes were summoned by a bell and began with prayer followed by the reading of the 'catalogue', the register. The Arts curriculum was nominally the same – Greek, some Latin, Logic and the elements of Arithmetic in the first two years; Ethics, Metaphysics, Arithmetic and Geometry in the third; Natural Philosophy in the fourth – but the content of classes changed to reflect a revived but Protestant scholasticism.

The majority of students were the sons of ministers, burgesses and farmers and there was an increasing number of bursars. But when they matriculated, and many seem not to have done so, significant numbers wrote proudly that they were the sons of earls, lords or lairds. In the ten years after 1675, for example, three were sons of the earl of Argyll and four of the duke of Hamilton. Increasingly students were seeking education and not preparing for the ministry. A significant new appointment was made in 1640. The four-year Divinity course had been the responsibility of the Principal himself but now a professor of Divinity was appointed. The title was a relatively new one for a teacher of a defined subject and this was Glasgow's first 'chair'. Further chairs were proposed but none were created. Money was scarce, regenting was restored in 1642 and recently created posts in law and medicine were discontinued. But education and scholarship were changing and in little more than a generation after 1691 eleven chairs were created. Life and teaching in the College changed radically and a new and very different period in the history of the University began.

Change began soon after the 'Glorious' Revolution of 1688–9 which drove out King James VII and II and brought William of

The Inner Court and the Tower of the Old College.

lodged in the College and in 1702 Principal Stirling reckoned that there were 323 Arts students and 'upwards of 400' when the students of theology were added. By 1800 there were well over a thousand. In 1694 the common table was abandoned. Some students were able to rent upper rooms in the College and, later, in professors' houses; some lived at home; but most found lodgings in the town to suit their means. The College became essentially a teaching building as in most other European universities.

In the eighteenth century fewer sons of the higher nobility came to Glasgow – if they went to university at all, they attended Oxford or Cambridge, but significant numbers continued to be the sons of lords and lairds. Most students were the sons of the 'middling' sort, ministers, professional men, merchants and farmers; over the century increasing numbers were the sons of the 'lower sort', weavers and workmen for example; and the common designation 'agricola' for a father's occupation must have covered a range of tenant 'farmer'. The 'raw-boned' lad from a country school, living very cheaply in a tenement room, perhaps relying on food sent up by carter from home, well-documented in the nineteenth century, must now have become common. Few could have been able to join the student clubs and societies or write for the ephemeral journals which became a feature of Glasgow student life or enjoy the social life of a city, growing fast and prosperous on the trade in sugar, distilling and tobacco. Most students still came from farms and small towns in west and south-west Scotland, Stirlingshire and Perthshire but from late in the century increasing numbers were the

Orange and Mary, James' daughter, to the thrones of both kingdoms. The disputes and violence that had marred the seventeenth century gradually died down; political and religious settlements were made; and in 1707, for the promise of better times, the kingdoms and parliaments of England and Scotland were united in one kingdom and one parliament. Student numbers rose. By 1695 no more than half the students could be sons of employers and workers in the expanding industries in and around Glasgow. Large numbers now came from Presbyterian Ireland, most from the areas of recent Scottish settlement in the north. Smaller numbers came from England and Wales, most dissenters deterred by religious tests at Oxford, Cambridge and Dublin. Episcopalians and Catholics came for there were no 'tests' until graduation and a Glasgow education was attractively cheap. Students from Europe came and links began with the Americas, often through Scottish settlers. David Campbell, bookseller in Boston, sent two books on Indian Languages to the Library in 1693 and further books followed. William Campbell from Jamaica matriculated in 1724, and an Anglo-Virginian and a Scot 'ex Maryland' are recorded in 1726. Later in the century, in spite of Glasgow's new reputation for scholarship, the numbers of Irish and overseas students declined because of the foundation of their own denominational colleges. A few English gentlemen came to Glasgow at the end of the century because the war with France denied them the Grand Tour. One, the future Prime Minister, Viscount Melbourne, came with his brother for two years, but, sadly, he said that it was 'the dirtiest (town) I ever saw'!

In spite of the greater numbers, rarely more than twenty students graduated in any year before 1760 and never more than forty before 1810. Graduations then increased, most in Medicine, and Arts graduates began to be numerous only late in the nineteenth century. A degree was not yet the key to a career; even intending ministers did not need to graduate in Arts or in Divinity. If

The Outer Court of the Old College with the Lion and Unicorn staircase leading to the Fore Hall.

evidence of attainment was required, 'class tickets' signed by professors or, better, the glory of a prize awarded by the votes of his fellow students would suffice. Many students attended classes for only a year or two and many were private students who had not matriculated. This was a better tradition than it may seem for higher education was offered to students who could not afford to attend the full degree course or had been sent by their fathers to be 'improved' before they were tied to the counting house or the office or the land. Standards were sometimes criticised as more appropriate to a school-room and indeed students who came better prepared, often English and Irish students, were permitted to enter the senior language classes and complete the degree in three years. It was a practical and economical education. The Scottish universities accepted that many parish schools in Scotland could achieve only a limited standard and offered students the chance to better it at modest cost. English classicists criticised them for devoting only two years to Latin and Greek and allowing some students to begin Greek with the alphabet, but this was compensated by two years of philosophy and science. Francis Jeffrey, an eminent Scottish lawyer who had been a student in Glasgow, answered criticism of the Scottish system in 1826. 'I think it is a great good on the whole, because it enables relatively large numbers of people to get – not indeed profound learning, for that is not to be spoken of – but that knowledge which tends to liberalise and make intelligent the mass of the population, more than anything else'. By then a third of Scottish dominies (schoolmasters) were said to have studied at a university and the

proportion of university-educated Scottish school teachers was unequalled elsewhere in Britain until the mid-twentieth century.

Jeffrey was correct but by the mid-eighteenth century Scotland had some remarkable and internationally acclaimed scholar professors. The first of the new Glasgow chairs, many funded by the Crown, was in Mathematics. It had been recommended by royal visitors in 1664 and was created in 1691. A Greek chair followed in 1704, then Humanity (Latin), Oriental Languages, Practice of Medicine, Law, Ecclesiastical History, and Anatomy and Botany between 1706 and 1718. And in 1727 the last regents were given their choice of chairs of Logic and Rhetoric, Moral Philosophy and Natural Philosophy. Most chairs were in the broad subjects of the old curriculum but some were in new or specialised fields. The Principal had been responsible for teaching Hebrew and Aramaic; this now passed to a Regius Professor of Oriental Languages. Ecclesiastical History or chronology had been part of Divinity but in 1691 William Jameson, a blind minister, was appointed to teach it and when he retired a Regius Chair of Ecclesiastical History was founded in 1716. The University itself undertook what was effectively a new venture in 1712 'Considering (that) the professions of law and medicine have of a long time been neglected in this university ... and that the reviving of the same would tend much to the advantage and honour of the society', and being assured by a letter from the rector that they could be financed from a fund established by King William III, it decided to found chairs in both subjects. The decision was timely because lectures on both subjects were now offered in other universities. Regius Chairs of Civil Law and Practice of Medicine were funded by Queen Anne in 1713 and the University itself funded a chair of Anatomy and Botany in 1718. The age of the professors had begun — literally so because they were almost the only teachers until the late nineteenth century.

The Arts classes taken by the majority of students remained traditional, at least in name. Graduation required two years of Latin and Greek, then Rhetoric (Logic) and Ethics (Moral Philosophy), Natural Philosophy including Mathematics, Physics, Astronomy and Geography. It was basically the same until 1893 and some of the old titles continued until the 1980s when Humanity became Latin, Moral Philosophy and Logic became Philosophy and Natural Philosophy became Physics. Teaching however changed radically. Latin was no longer a working language for most students and by the mid-eighteenth century almost all teaching was in English – or Scots. Regenting ended in 1727 and professors lectured on the subject they professed though with a wide discretion on the syllabus. A few were disappointing; most were conscientious; and a number were distinguished in a century in which Scottish scholarship became famous. Francis Hutcheson, a Glasgow graduate, Professor of Moral Philosophy from 1730 to 1746, is an example of the 'enlightened' teacher who succeeded in enthusing students to think and express themselves. He lectured in English, 'three days a week on classical sources, five days on natural Religion, Morals, Jurisprudence, and Government'. He held regular meetings of his class to question students on their comprehen-

sion, take part in disputations and hear essays read out – and these might run to tens of foolscap pages! Hutcheson was a good scholar and he had a number of distinguished pupils. One was Adam Smith, the 'father' of Political Economy, who came to the University aged fourteen in 1737 and returned to teach from 1751 to 1764, as professor of Logic and then of Moral Philosophy. His Moral Philosophy class covered natural theology, ethics, jurisprudence and economics. From these came the original ideas in his *The Theory of Moral Sentiments* published in 1759 and *The Wealth of Nations* in 1776, still the classic text in economics. As a Nobel Prizeman expressed it a few years ago, 'Adam Smith is alive and well and living in Chicago'. He is in fact buried in the Canongate churchyard in Edinburgh. John Millar, another of Hutcheson's students, entered the University at the age of eleven, spent at least six years as a student and became the very successful Professor of Law from 1761 to 1801. He lectured to numbers of students on Roman Law, Jurisprudence, Government and Scots and English Law and wrote on government and society. His four-volume *Historical View of English Government* is a remarkably original book which covers a number of modern disciplines. Striking material evidence of the new scholarship is the bookshop and printing press carried on in the College by the brothers Robert and Andrew Foulis for over thirty years from 1740. As 'Printers to the University' they published over 500 items including fine editions of many Greek and Latin classics. They also founded an Academy of Arts to exhibit pictures (sometimes in the open in the College quadrangles) and teach young artists, and continued it, not very successfully, for over twenty years.

The change in the University was due in part to change in the city of Glasgow which was growing in size and becoming more prosperous, more open and lively. There were gentlemen's clubs and societies such as the Political Economy Club and the Glasgow Literary Society in which professors took an active part. Some professors gave public lectures. Francis Hutcheson gave free Sunday evening lectures which drew large crowds. Both William Cullen and Joseph Black, the first lecturers in Chemistry, opened their classes to men who were interested in the new science or might benefit in their business. John Anderson, 'Jolly Jack Phosphorus', professor of Natural Philosophy from 1757 to 1796 and constantly in dispute with his colleagues, carried this further. His class in experimental philosophy was open to the public and he encouraged workmen and mechanics to attend, offering 'tickets' enabling them to attend without fee. In his will he left money to found a university 'for the good of mankind and the improvement of science' and, far ahead of his time, open to 'the ladies of Glasgow'. The money was inadequate for the purpose but an Andersonian Institution was created and eventually flourished as the Royal Technical College (RTC) and since 1964 as the University of Strathclyde (page 111).

The University to-day has much more in common with the university of the eighteenth century than with the earlier College but the similarity in terminology can be misleading. There has been vast change since 1700 and none so rapid as in the last half century. The time-scale of change in teaching and research is clearest in the sciences. They had been transformed in the seventeenth century. For example the Royal Society was founded in London in 1661; Newton's *Principia* published in 1687; and the importance of experiment and apparatus recognised. Astronomy is a good example of the change in Glasgow. It had been taught since 1451 when the principal teaching text was the *Sphere* compiled by John of Holywood, a thirteenth-century English cleric, on the basis of texts written by Greek and Arab writers over more than a thousand years. In the sixteenth century observational and mathematical work throughout Europe began a revolution in astronomy and in Glasgow, though the *Sphere* continued to be used for a time, teaching slowly changed. Some time before 1689 the University had acquired a telescope five feet long and in 1693 it paid or sought £32 for 'ane telescope eight feet long, ane prisma and twelve tubes for weather glasses' – barometers. It had been debating for some time how to fund an observatory when in 1754 Alexander Macfarlane, merchant in Jamaica, bequeathed it the instruments in his observatory. They were damaged on the voyage but a young technician, James Watt, the later inventor, recently returned from training as an instrument-maker in London, was able to rescue them.* The Macfarlane Observatory was opened in the College grounds in 1757 and in 1760 George II funded a chair of Practical Astronomy. The professor's primary duty was to observe and publish the results and from the mid-nineteenth century Glasgow astronomy began to be notable in both teaching and observational research. The second half of the twentieth century has

---

* Watt was given a room in the College and styled himself mathematical instrument maker to the University. It was there, with the help of John Anderson, professor of Natural Philosophy, that he first experimented on the properties of steam engines.

however been the age of space exploration and vastly expensive earthbound equipment. There is still a University Observatory in Glasgow, the third since 1757 as it was moved westwards to escape the polluted atmosphere of the industrial city – but it is now used primarily for teaching. In 1986 the decision was taken to unite the Chairs and the departments of Natural Philosophy and Astronomy as Physics and Astronomy. The range of classes and honours degrees in Astronomy and Mathematics or Physics however continues and a research group in Astronomy and Astrophysics flourishes.

Other branches of Science developed on a similar time scale. By the early 1700s instruments and materials were provided for Natural Philosophy, and the professor was required to conduct a practical course in 'experimental philosophy'. A lectureship in Chemistry was created in 1747 to support the teaching of Medicine and equipment was provided for the laboratory where in the 1760s Joseph Black, a Glasgow student, Professor of Anatomy and Botany and then of Practice of Medicine, made the first major scientific discoveries in the University – on latent heat. In 1818 a chair of Chemistry in the Medical Faculty was founded and in 1831 a laboratory and classrooms for Chemistry were built in Shuttle Street, near the College, probably the first building of its kind in the world. When the University moved to Gilmorehill in 1870 an octagonal laboratory, said to be modelled on the medieval Abbot's Kitchen at Glastonbury, was built for Chemistry and this with some hutted buildings had to suffice until 1940 when the first part of a new Chemistry building was opened. Small by to-day's standards, it was considered then 'the finest and best equipped department in the UK'. In 1870 the teaching of Chemistry was the responsibility of the professor himself and even in 1920 there were only a professor, two lecturers (for women students and medical students) and four assistants or demonstrators in Chemistry. By 1940 there were three professors and fifteen lecturers. To-day, in recently enlarged and reconditioned buildings there are eight professors, sixteen readers, fourteen lecturers, and a large number of associated academics, technicians and support staff. Glasgow has a fine collection of old scientific instruments, some on display in the Hunterian Museum, to illustrate the change. One striking example is the contrast between the very basic equipment used by Glasgow's greatest nineteenth-century scientist, William Thomson, Lord Kelvin, Professor of Natural Philosophy from 1846 until 1899, and the massive facilities provided for the department over the last half century beginning with the electron synchrotron of 1954.

The teaching of medicine authorised by the bull of 1451 also began in the eighteenth century. It had been offered between 1637 and 1646 but it was not until 1714 that the University, influenced by contemporary views of the importance of medical instruction, appointed a professor of Practice of Medicine to a chair funded by the crown. The modern medical school effectively began when William Cullen, the most outstanding clinical teacher of his day, was appointed to the chair in 1751; though both he and Joseph Black, the chemist, were later tempted away to Edinburgh where bedside instruction was possible in the Royal Infirmary. In Glasgow teaching was carried out in the infirmary of the Town's Hospital opened in 1740 on the banks of the Clyde; but it was the foundation in 1794 of the Glasgow Royal Infirmary beside the Cathedral and close to the University that provided teaching facilities to equal those in Edinburgh. Glasgow quickly established itself as a principal centre for medical education within the United Kingdom. Student numbers grew rapidly during the French wars to train doctors to serve with the armed forces and by 1810 there were some 300 medical students from all parts of Britain. Many still used the university medical classes to complement their training as apprentices and the high flyers moved around the medical schools to learn from the best practitioners of the day. The number of MDs awarded rose sharply, in part because the other Scottish Universities had tightened their regulations which now included compulsory Latin!

The development of the medical school owed much to a determined group of pioneers. The brothers Allan and John Burns were skilful anatomists. John introduced surgery, essential in military service where amputations were common, into the curriculum and became the first professor of Surgery in 1815. In the same year James Towers became the first professor of Midwifery and laid the foundations of hospital maternity care in the City. Further chairs in Materia Medica, Physiology and Forensic Medicine were established by the Crown in the 1830s, sometimes against the wishes of the other professors. This was a niggling period in the history of the College. There was a long and bitter dispute with the Faculty of Physicians and Surgeons in Glasgow founded in 1599 over the right to license doctors to practise and this was not resolved until the Medical Act of 1858 regulated entry into the profession and required all practitioners to register with the newly formed General Medical Council. Student numbers also declined because the need for military doctors fell and medical training became more widely available elsewhere. A major change began with the appointment of Joseph Lister as professor of Surgery in 1860. Within four years he was experimenting with the use of carbolic acid to prevent the spread of infection in wounds, the main cause of the many post-operative deaths. After several trials, the first patient to be successfully treated for a compound fracture (where the bone perforated the skin) was James Greenlees in August 1865. This achievement placed Glasgow at the forefront of modern surgery, a position which it maintained into the twentieth century. The growth of the medical school owed much to the close proximity of the College and the Royal Infirmary and when the University moved to Gilmorehill in 1870 a new hospital, the Western Infirmary, was built beside it and the Medical chairs transferred there. Disappointed, the Royal established its own St Mungo's College of Medicine and relations with the University did not resume until the first decade of the twentieth century when the Muirhead and other chairs were founded (page 96).

Law, taught continuously from the foundation of the chair in 1713, developed quite differently and had no professional degree until 1878. The chair was in Civil Law but in practice most early professors lectured on

Civil and Scots Law and offered additional courses at additional fees on other branches of law, sometimes varying the topics from year to year. But only some fifty law degrees were conferred before 1800, all but one LL.D.s and often as an honorary degree. Glasgow lawyers continued to qualify by apprenticeship and admission to practise after examination by the local Faculty of Procurators but the university classes were a boon to apprentices and writers' clerks who did not intend to graduate. Numbers varied directly with the quality of the teaching. John Millar (1761–1801) was an outstanding teacher and scholar, but his successor, Robert

Davidson, who held the Chair until 1841, had no students at all in some early years. In 1861 the Faculty of Procurators, encouraged by increasing numbers attending classes, funded a second law chair in Conveyancing and in 1862 a three-year LL.B. degree was introduced. It was, however, open only to Arts graduates; it was not a professional qualification and, not surprisingly, it attracted few students. In 1878 a two-year, later three-year B.L. first degree was created with lectures at 8 a.m. in the University at Gilmorehill and 5.30 p.m. in the Hall of the Faculty of Procurators in the city for the benefit of apprentices in law offices. Student numbers increased to around 200 by 1900, 400 in the 1930s and over 600 in the 1950s and the number of graduates rose. It was only in 1961, after

The new Library completed in 1782 with the Hamilton Building behind.

much debate and doubt, that a full-time first degree, the LL.B., wholly taught in the University, was introduced. Since then the degree and a further university year studying legal practice has become the normal entry to the profession. Increasing academic study of law and vastly greater state funding for universities and students in the 1960s had made possible the transformation of legal studies in the University.

The new seventeenth-century College buildings were scarcely complete before growing student numbers from the 1690s and changes in teaching made first adaptation and later new building essential. Residence and the common life was abandoned and walls and partitions were taken down to give each professor a lecture room with a retiring room or cramped space for experiments and demonstrations. The low ceilings, the relatively small rooms and the narrow stairs became increasingly inconvenient and eventually the east range of the east quadrangle was demolished and replaced in 1811 by the architecturally very different but more spacious and better-lit Hamilton Building funded by a bequest from John Hamilton, merchant in Canton. An archway from it led east into the new Museum Square. On the far side was the fine Hunterian Museum designed by William Stark and completed in 1804 to house the magnificent collection of books, manuscripts, coins, medical materials and other items bequeathed to the University in 1783 by William Hunter.* On the south

The Hunterian Museum at the Old College.

side there was a new Library completed in 1782. And behind the Museum, the College gardens stretched to the Molendinar Burn, beyond to the Observatory and to a large area of open ground where students played games and snow-balled and, on one infamous occasion in 1810, fought a pitched battle with soldiers of the 71st Regiment of Foot. South of the College, beyond the University Physic Garden, a new Blackfriars Church replaced the medieval church struck by lightning and destroyed by fire in 1670 but the University ended its connection with Blackfriars in 1764 when the new church was in danger of collapse and from then on Sunday services were normally held in a hall in the University.

Immediately north of the College another quadrangle, the Professors' Court, with a carriage entrance from the High Street was begun in 1722 and by 1780 it had eleven terrace houses. The Principal and all thirteen professors now had houses in the College or the Court. This proved both a bond and a source of friction, particularly over the allocation and repair of the houses, and for fifty years from 1807 provoked an 'issue' worthy of Trollope's Barchester. It began when the Crown, without consulting the University, founded a Chair in Natural History (Zoology), the first new chair since 1760, and appointed to it Lockhart Muirhead, the College Librarian, who was already teaching the subject. A majority of the professors took the issue of his status to the Court of Session which decided in 1808 that while Muirhead was properly a professor in the University,

---

* William Hunter from East Kilbride, near Glasgow, was an Arts student in the University from 1731 to 1736. He was then apprenticed to a local doctor, attended medical classes in Edinburgh for two years and made a very successful career in London in midwifery, anatomy and surgery. He died in 1783 and bequeathed his great collection of art and artefacts to the University with £8,000 to build a Museum to house them.

The eighteenth-century Professors' Court.

he was not entitled 'to infringe upon or participate in the patronage and patrimonial and other rights of the present professors of the College of Glasgow'. This was a dire decision. It meant that the holders of new chairs, and eight were created between 1807 and 1840, were members of the Senate but not of the Faculty where financial and academic decisions were taken and had no right to a professorial house, access to the library or to benefit in any way from the endowments, ironically most of them provided by the Crown. The distinction was condemned by a Royal Commission on the Scottish Universities appointed in 1826 but no action was taken by

government until 1858 when the Universities (Scotland) Act placed all professors on an equal footing save that the sole right of the 'ancient' professors to the houses remained. In 1870 twelve houses were built for them in a Professors' Court or Square at Gilmorehill – the professor of Astronomy lived beside the Observatory. After 1945 these five-storey houses became less attractive; holders of other chairs were permitted to rent them; and more recently they have been adapted for teaching and administration. Now only the Principal has a residence.

The last seventy years of the University on the High Street before the move to Gilmorehill in 1870 saw new chairs and new subjects created and the University receive a new constitution which is still the basis of its form of government. The Crown created eight new chairs between 1807 and 1840. Five, Surgery, Midwifery, Materia Medica, Theory of Physics (Physiology) and Forensic Medicine, were in Medicine and two, Botany and Chemistry, were placed in the Medical Faculty (page 22). And in 1840, to the displeasure of many professors, Queen Victoria founded a Chair in Civil Engineering and Mechanics, the first engineering chair in Britain. It was assigned to the Faculty of Arts, reluctantly given attic accommodation and classes began. Some of its professors were professionally distinguished but student numbers were small, even when a B.Sc. degree introduced in 1872 permitted specialisation in engineering. It was only late in the century, when Glasgow became a great engineering centre and the 'Second City of the Empire', and a second chair, Naval Architecture, was endowed that the status of Engineering in the University was accepted, though it became a Faculty only in 1923. The Commissioners appointed by the 1858 Act made attendance on a class in English necessary for the Arts degree and in 1861 the Crown founded chairs in English Literature, the first new 'Arts' chair since 1727, and in Divinity and Biblical Criticism and the Glasgow Faculty of Procurators helped endow the chair of Conveyancing.

It was still a university of professors. They were almost the only teachers and they enjoyed a great deal of freedom in what and how they taught. Most were able and conscientious but very conscious of their status

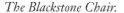

The Blackstone Chair.

and rights. Each had an annual stipend from the University or the Crown and until 1893 collected and retained the class fees paid by their students. This meant great disparities in their income and teaching load. Some were tempted to cling over-long to their chairs – a retiring age of 70 was introduced only in 1897 – and some employed younger men to assist them. There were well-founded allegations of nepotism and overt political patronage in some appointments, dogged defence of subjects and resistance to new ones. Yet in 1826 they reviewed the Arts curriculum. The graduation curriculum was not modified but sensible changes were made. A small number of B.A. degrees had been awarded since 1774 and it was now formally provided that students who passed examinations in Latin, Greek, Logic and Moral Philosophy might graduate B.A. in three years or, if they passed additionally in Mathematics and Natural Philosophy, M.A. in four years. About 350 B.A.s and more than 500 M.A.s were awarded between 1826 and the abolition of the B.A. degree by the 1858 Act. The 1826 review also provided the first Honours M.A. degrees in Classics and Philosophy or Mathematics and Natural Philosophy. They required passes in all the traditional subjects and extended study in the chosen area, in practice by attending a further class in the subjects. Only small numbers took the degree and Honours teaching and examining as it exists to-day developed only slowly from the late nineteenth century but the principle was accepted.

After 1858 the traditional method of examination, questioning the candidate on the Blackstone Chair as long as sand ran in the glass, was replaced by written examination papers. The subjects of questions are familiar but, by to-day's standards, they demanded excessively factual answers to over-many questions. The professors' lecture notes must have been the basis of most of the answers! This is not to disparage the professors nor the students. Professors of degree subjects had to lecture five days a week to meet the requirement of a hundred lectures in the twenty weeks of term between mid-November and the end of March and conduct translation, disputation or practical classes as well. Some professors had both senior and junior classes. A twenty-week session seems short now but it was longer than that of the other Scottish universities and the long vacation enabled students to earn money to support them in the following year – and helped attract distinguished professors to Glasgow (page 93).

The 1858 Act gave all the Scottish universities a more balanced and effective system of government and ended the rule of the Faculty in Glasgow. The Senate, that is the Principal and all professors, became responsible for the finances, the administration of the property and revenues of the University and for teaching and discipline; while a new body, the University Court, was given power to review decisions of the Senate, nominate professors other than the Regius professors, and ensure that professors and the Principal carried out their duties. The 1889 Universities (Scotland) Act, still the basis of the government of the University to-day, was more

The Bedellus leading the Principal and the Professors down the Lion and Unicorn staircase in the Old College for the last time.

Jemima Blackburn's painting of the removal of the contents of the Hunterian Museum, 1870.

radical, giving the Senate responsibility for academic matters and the Court authority in finance, fabric and appointments, but 1858 was the end of an era. The 1858 University Court consisted of seven members reflecting a range of interests – the Rector elected by the students, the Principal, the Dean of Faculties elected by the Senate, and four assessors chosen respectively by the Chancellor, the Rector, the Senate and the General Council. The last was also a new body composed of all graduates in Arts and Medicine over 21, all professors, the chancellor and a few others, meeting twice a year to receive reports on the University and with the right to elect the Chancellor. The government of the University but little else had changed. In 1858 the thousand or so students were taught by twenty-two professors with the aid of a

of the city. The old buildings were too small for student numbers, the lecture rooms were inadequate and the fabric was decaying. There was more than enough land to rebuild on the same site and east of the Molendinar Burn, but the teeming population, the decay of the houses and industrial pollution was making the High Street increasingly unpleasant and the Molendinar Burn was now a reeking, enclosed sewer. An opportunity seemed to have come in 1845 when a railway company offered to buy the entire College site and build a new College on Woodlands Hill, across Kelvingrove Park from the present University. It even offered to build and provide support for a new hospital to compensate for the loss of teaching facilities in the Royal Infirmary on the High Street. Plans and designs were prepared but by 1849 it was clear that the Company was unable to fund them and the University had to be content with £10,000 compensation to open a Fabric Fund. Discussion continued until 1863 when the Glasgow Union Railway Company offered £100,000 for the College site with occupation in five years. This was promptly accepted and the forty-three-acre site at Gilmorehill bought for £65,000. Building, funded by the sale of the Old College, a Treasury grant and public subscriptions took longer than expected but on 29 July 1870 the Senate formally left the College and on the following day the Railway Company took possession of the site which had been the home of the University for more than four hundred years. There was sadness to see the Old College converted into a railway station and home for small businesses and then demolished; but the intention was to continue the old traditions and methods in the new buildings at Gilmorehill.

few assistants they appointed. There were a handful of librarians and servitors but scarcely any administrators. There was little public funding; but already a great deal of government intervention.

One issue on which most professors were agreed by the 1840s was the disadvantages of the College buildings on the High Street and the advantages of moving to new buildings on the developing but respectable west side

CHAPTER 2

The University at Gilmorehill, 1870–1996

The new buildings at Gilmorehill were formally opened by the Chancellor, the Duke of Montrose, on 7 November, 1870. They followed the plan of the Old College but on a grander scale and a Gothic style. There were east and west quadrangles, turret staircases in the east quadrangle and houses for the Principal and twelve 'ancient' professors in an adjoining square. Each non-clinical professor had his lecture-room with a retiring-room or a modest laboratory. The Library and the Hunterian Museum were complete but lack of money meant that the west side of the west quadrangle, the 'cloisters' dividing the quadrangles with the great Hall above, and the spire on the tower had not been built and the new teaching hospital, the Western Infirmary, did not open until 1874. The generosity of the Marquess of Bute and Charles Randolph enabled the Hall and its grand staircase to be completed in 1882, the spire was added in 1883, but the west quadrangle was not completed until 1929 and on a different plan and style. There were

almost 1,300 students in four Faculties (Theology, Arts, Medicine and Law) in 1870, about the same number as in 1800, but only 160 graduated in 1871 – 106 in Medicine and 37 in Arts. The staff consisted of the Principal, twenty-five professors, one lecturer in diseases of the eye, nine professors' assistants annually appointed, a Registrar who served as assistant Clerk of Senate, a Librarian and two assistants, a Bedellus and four janitors. In 1996 on the Gilmorehill campus, now more than twice the size, and at Garscube there are over 14,000 undergraduates and over 3,200 postgraduates in eight faculties and almost 4,300 graduated in 1995. There are over 100 departments, almost 120 professorial chairs, 1,100 other academics, 620 full-time research staff, 350 administrators and 1,700 support staff.

Top right: South elevation of the new University building, 1870.

Bottom right: The east side of the new University taking shape, 1868.

Student numbers grew in stages. By 1880, mainly because of increasing prosperity in the west of Scotland, there were 2,300 students – 1,406 in Arts and 563 in Medicine. Arts numbers fell back heavily during a recession in the 1890s but by 1914 there were 1,250 students in Arts, 550 in Science and over 800 in Medicine – almost 3,000 in all, and, significantly, almost 550 graduated. Prosperity had returned. More important, there were now 647 women students, 499 in Arts, 109 in medicine, 39 in Science, though none in Law or Theology. A campaign for the higher education of women had begun in Glasgow in the 1860s and in 1877 the Glasgow Association for the Higher Education for

Women had been formed under the dynamic leadership of Mrs Jessie Campbell of Tullichewen near Loch Lomond with the enthusiastic support of Principal John Caird. In 1884 Queen Margaret College for women was opened in North Park House gifted by Mrs Isabella Elder, the widow of a wealthy shipbuilder. It was not far from the University and some university professors assisted in the teaching. In 1892 the University Commissioners appointed under the 1889 Universities (Scotland) Act opened the universities in Scotland to women. In Glasgow 131 women were at once admitted; the union of the College and the University soon followed; and in 1894 Marion Gilchrist became the

Left: The contractors, masons and workmen at Gilmorehill, 1868.

Below: Erecting the staging for the ceremony of laying the foundation stone, 1868.

first woman graduate of the University – with high commendation in Medicine. By 1900 there were almost 350 women students and their numbers grew as the University expanded. It was, however, only in the 1960s that the proportion of women began to rise steadily, then more rapid in the 1970s and in 1995 for the first time, half the full-time students were women. In 1935 the University sold the College building, which was no longer required for teaching and it became the home of the BBC in Scotland.

A Science Faculty was created in 1893 from subjects previously in Arts and Medicine and this also led to growing student numbers, particularly after 1900 when the sciences achieved a new status and dedicated buildings with modern facilities were built for some of them west of the Professors' Square. The demand for school teachers also brought more students. From 1872 Scotland had a national

Elevation of the south front of the Scott building.

system of schools funded by local authorities under the control of the Scotch Education Department. Teacher-training expanded and some of the best students attended university classes during the winter months. They began to gain diplomas, then degrees and by 1900 most of the male students were attending university classes. In 1906 this was recognised in historic and uniquely Scottish regulations that while graduates with an Ordinary degree could become primary teachers after a year in training college, secondary teachers must have studied their teaching subject for at least two years in university followed by a year in college. This encouraged students, particularly women, to come to university and until the 1960s teaching was the most common career for Arts and Science graduates. After the First World War special programmes for ex-service men led to increased numbers, particularly in Science, and by 1921 there were 4,800 students. Primarily because of the economic depression numbers then fluctuated

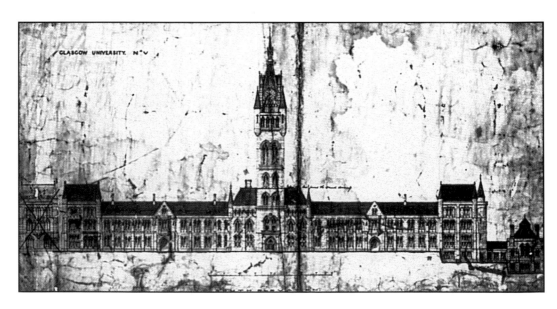

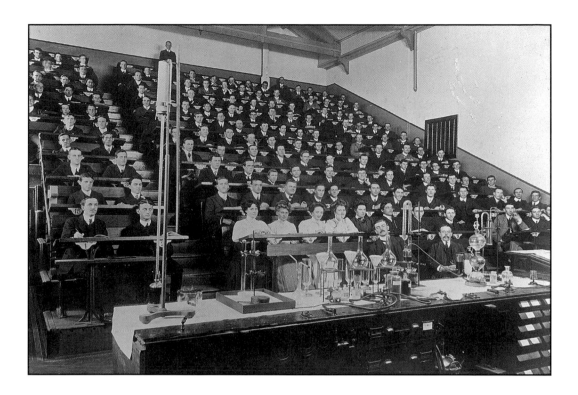

Chemistry lecture theatre in about 1900.

fluctuated between 4,500 and 5,500 until the outbreak of war in 1939 but Honours degrees became more common. The return of service men and women from 1945 led to a rise to 7,500 and then a fall to 6,000 students in the 1950s. Unprecedented and now state-funded expansion of higher education in Britain followed the recommendation of the Robbins Committee in 1963 that 'courses of higher education should be available for all those who are qualified by ability and attainment to pursue them and who wish to do so'. By 1974 the University had 10,000 students and demand and national policy has increased this to 17,679 students, excluding those in associated colleges in 1995, over 3,200 of them postgraduates. Doctorates had been offered in all subjects since 1908 and Ph.D.s since 1919, but it was after 1945 that research student numbers increased rapidly,

particularly in the sciences and medicine as posts in universities and research laboratories became more plentiful. And from the 1980s the demands of employers have led to a considerable increase in the range and variety of research and second degrees and qualifications in all faculties.

Growth in student numbers before increased funding by government in the 1960s was possible only because staffing and costs were low. Teaching was often in large classes and fees were held low. In 1920 the inclusive annual student fee was ten guineas (£10.50) in Arts and fifteen guineas in Science; in 1961 £35 in Arts, £55 in Science. There were modest university and local authority bursaries and grants for students and, very

Queen Margaret College Medical Building, 1890.

Queen Margaret College Entrance Hall, 1890.

Queen Margaret College Mistress's Office, 1890.

Queen Margaret College Chemical Laboratory, 1890.

Queen Margaret Union at Gilmorehill in the 1960s.

importantly, from 1901 the Carnegie Trust in Scotland gave grants to a good many Scottish students to assist with fees. Students with limited means were able to come to the University though it was often a struggle for them and their families. Glasgow had the advantage that it was at the heart of a region with over 40 per cent of the Scottish population and a high proportion of students could live at home. Many travelled in by train every day and it was common for them to walk long distances within the city to save tram fares. If travel was impossible there were relatively cheap lodgings in family tenement flats near the University and few student residences were built until the 1960s. Since then the University has become more cosmopolitan. In 1962 over 90 per cent of its students were from Scotland, over 73 per cent from within 30 miles of Glasgow; less than 4 per cent from the rest of the UK and less than 6 per cent from beyond. In the early 1980s the number of local students began to decline but this was more than compensated by students from the rest of Scotland, the rest of the UK and overseas. In 1996 70 per cent of full-time students are from Scotland but only 44 per cent come from within 30 miles of Glasgow; 17 per cent from the rest of the UK and 13 per cent from beyond. Diversity has enhanced the University, but at a cost. More residences had to be built and since 1983 £24 million has been borrowed to do so. There are now over 4,000 student places in university halls of residence, flats or rented accommodation and the latest residential development is a 'Student Village' for more than 1,000 students with shops and a doctor's surgery at Maryhill, a mile from the University.

Trams at the terminus at the foot of University Avenue in the 1950s.

The Glasgow student has changed a great deal since 1870, particularly since the expansion of higher education and the introduction of student maintenance grants in the 1960s. In the 1950s the traditional red undergraduate gowns were still worn by a few students, mainly women, but by the 1960s even university blazers became rare! Jeans and T-shirts became ubiquitous. The two student Unions, clubs which have played such an important part in student life, the Glasgow University Union for men founded in 1885 and the Queen Margaret Union for women founded in 1906, voted in 1980 to became 'mixed'. Single-sex student catering halls of residence were the norm in the 1960s; now the greatest demand is for self-catering flats. Teaching has become increasing informal. Few lecturers wear gowns and they are likely to know their Honours students by their first names. Some students even address younger lecturers in the

way! Students have become much more temperate. Early this century graduations were often riotous with broken heads and benches and singing before lectures; stamping at late-comers and shouted witticisms were common until 1939. Some lecturers might be intimidated but most professors could produce silence by a glance or a remark and a few were said to cure a persistent cough by a silent stare! Many students were unable to afford time or money to take much part in student activities but some 'professional' students spent years 'enjoying' the university. There was a wildness which is no longer accepted. For example the poll to elect a rector every three years began with an approved 'fight', a scrum, between the supporters of the candidates to deny opponents access

Information retrieval today.

Electronic music laboratory, 1993.

through a partially open quadrangle door to the poll where voting was by public declaration, the method used until 1872 at parliamentary elections. The fight ceased in 1953 and voting is now by secret ballot. The traditional Charities Day, when students took to the streets in fancy dress to collect money, is no longer held but students are still generous in giving and collecting for charities and assisting with social projects.

Greater government funding in the 1960s led to major changes in teaching. In 1870 the professors did most of the formal teaching. In degree classes they lectured daily and where tutorial teaching was given, it was in meetings of the full class. A cautious, slow expansion in the number of teachers and teaching subjects began after 1900 and by 1950 there were over 200 non-clinical lecturers and many untenured assistants who marked essays and

essays and examinations, gave short tutorials and took part in laboratory classes. It was still however common for professors to lecture to their first-year classes. Increased funding from the 1960s permitted a great expansion of staff and the creation of a diversity of Honours classes. Seminar and tutorial teaching became common, along with the greater use of benchwork in laboratories. Since then equipment, visual materials, television and now computing in special applications to teaching are in common use and the division between undergraduate and post-graduate work is lessening. The content and methods of teaching are now very much the same as in other large British universities. One important difference remains in the large, non-professional faculties, Arts, Science and Social Sciences. Students are still admitted to a Faculty not a Department, and they do not specialise immediately. In their first and second years they study a number of subjects and are taught in large lecture classes supported by seminars, tutorials, laboratories and field work. These more general years permit breadth of study, the opportunity to try new subjects and perhaps change direction – and about a third of students in these faculties do change their minds. They may graduate with a general (Ordinary) degree in three years or an Honours degree in four, specialising in one or two subjects over the final two years.

The majority of students in Science have taken Honours degrees since 1953; in Arts only since 1981; and now the overwhelming majority in both do so.

The range of disciplines and subjects has grown. In 1870 there were four faculties, Arts, Theology, Medicine and Law. Four more have been added – Science in 1893,

Graduation Ceremony in the Bute Hall.

Engineering in 1923, Veterinary Medicine in 1966 and Social Sciences in 1977. Professional degrees are awarded in Dentistry, Nursing Studies and Accountancy and there are many specialised research units. Within faculties there are now almost 120 departments. For example in Engineering there are Civil, Aeronautical, Mechanical, Naval and Ocean, and Electronics and Electrical Engineering. Within departments there are many units and recognised specialisms. There have also been affiliations and agreements with other institutions. In 1913 the RTC in Glasgow, descended from Anderson's College (page 20), was affiliated and Glasgow University degrees were awarded to its Science and Engineering students until 1964 when the College became the University of Strathclyde. There have been agreements to validate courses, share teaching and, more recently, to form partnerships. From 1930 to 1952 the Professor of Music was also Director of the Royal Scottish Academy of Music and Drama. Degrees are awarded to Glasgow School of Art students of Fine Art and Design, Architecture (where the head of the Mackintosh School is the University Professor of Architecture) and Product Design Engineering taught in both the School and the University. There is a long-standing validation and co-operative association with the Scottish College of Agriculture. Recently there have been associations and award of degrees to students of St Andrew's College of Education and of the National Board and local Colleges of Nursing and Midwifery. The University has become a very large and diverse institution, the largest in Scotland and the fifth largest in the United Kingdom.

Since the eighteenth century it has been common for professors to write scholarly books, edit texts and conduct scientific investigations in laboratories and observatories. In the twentieth century and particularly in the last fifty years the scale and the cost of 'research' has increased greatly, particularly in the sciences. Research has become not merely a personal endeavour but an obligation on every university teacher, often as part of a team and now subject to regular external monitoring. The scale and cost of research in the Sciences has grown immensely. For example, following wartime research, a large team was assembled in Natural Philosophy (Physics) in 1945 to work with government funding on nuclear physics using an electron synchrotron and a high-tension accelerator and a new building was built for the department. Since then research groups have became common in science, engineering, medicine and veterinary medicine. Large computing facilities have been provided and the Library, sometimes described as the Arts-side laboratory though in fact equally a Science-side resource, has been greatly expanded. The 1870 Library in the west quadrangle had to suffice until 1968 when the first phase of a towered Library, designed to balance visually the University tower, was opened across University Avenue. A second phase was added in 1982–3 and a third in 1986.

The great expansion in student and staff numbers, in degrees and courses, and the increased specialisation and scale of research has led to a transformation of the campus. In 1870 the main building and the Professors' Square were surrounded by lawns and playing fields but soon after 1900 many of many of the open areas were sacrificed for Medical, Science and Engineering buildings and in 1929 the open west side of the West Quadrangle was completed by the Chapel and an Arts building. There was now little vacant land on the original site and building began on the north side of University Avenue – in 1931 the Glasgow University (Men's) Union and in 1939 the Round Reading Room. In 1945 a University development zone was designated there and almost all the properties in an extended strip of land north of University Avenue were bought and adapted or replaced for university use. The area of the campus was almost trebled and specialised buildings such as the Stevenson Building for Physical Education, the new Library, the Refectory and the 'Hub' complex for staff and students, the Adam Smith Building for Social Sciences and the

and the Boyd-Orr Building for first-year Science teaching – often more utilitarian than beautiful – were constructed. The 1870 buildings are still used for teaching, for examinations, to house the Hunterian Museum but increasingly for administration. There are several field stations but the only area which can be called a 'second' campus is the Garscube estate, two miles from Gilmorehill, housing the Faculty of Veterinary Medicine, the Beatson Institute for Cancer Research, the Kelvin Conference Centre and the Wolfson Hall student residence. The great and unusual good fortune of the University is that it is still able to house almost all its teaching and most of its research on one site – at Gilmorehill.

The 'Rectorial fight', 1950.

UNIVERSITY UNION, G

46

CHAPTER 3

Building the modern University

Even in its unfinished state the new university building dominating Gilmorehill was magnificent, the largest public building to be constructed in Britain since the Houses of Parliament were completed in 1860. Designed by the English architect Gilbert Scott to the annoyance of Glasgow architects, it was arranged around two quadrangles like the Old College. Access to the lecture theatres in the east quadrangle was by turret staircases that bore a close resemblance to those in the High Street. Scott had been so impressed by the simplicity of the old building that, at the farewell dinner, he alone called for its preservation, at least in part. The architectural style of the new building, unusually for Glasgow with its classical tradition, was emphatically Gothic but the building technique was entirely modern, with extensive use of concrete, cast and wrought-iron columns and beams, and cast-iron windows. The facades from all perspectives were intended to give an impression of grandeur and solidity and the south front looking out across Kelvingrove Park was particularly imposing.

The east quadrangle was the home largely of the science and medical departments with law and divinity classrooms on the south front. The Chemistry laboratory just to the east of the south front was modelled on the Abbot's Kitchen at Glastonbury to designs favoured by the celebrated chemist Lavoisier. The west quadrangle housed Arts, which still included Mathematics and Natural Philosophy with their classrooms and laboratories. The Senate room and the imposing office of the Clerk of Senate, the only administrative office in the building, was under the tower. The central section of the north front contained the Library and Hunterian Museum. The lecture rooms, the largest with seating for two hundred, were equipped with tiers of wooden benches, imposing platforms, demonstration benches

The original McIntyre building, 1888.

and huge blackboards, and each professor had a retiring room to prepare for lectures and see individual students. There were thirteen rather gaunt houses for the Principal and professors of the original foundation arranged around an open square facing the uncompleted west quadrangle. And in 1872 the Lion and Unicorn staircase that had led to the Fore Hall of the Old College was reconstructed to give access from the Professors' Square to the West Quadrangle.

Apart from the purchase of the land, it was estimated at the outset that the cost of the new buildings would be well over £250,000. Neither Principal Barclay nor the senior Professor John Caird, whose previous careers had been entirely devoted to the parochial ministry, had any experience of raising money on this scale, but assisted by James A Campbell, owner of a Glasgow department store, and members of the General Council, they set about this formidable task, holding public meetings throughout the west of Scotland and as far afield as Manchester and London. The project quickly caught the public imagination. By 1868 subscriptions totalled £113,000 and the University had no difficulty in matching a generous Treasury grant of £120,000. Glasgow's enthusiasm for the new building was demonstrated by the crowd of over twenty thousand which attended the laying of the foundation stone by the Prince and Princess of Wales on 8 October 1868. The brass plates commemorating this event can be seen in the entrance hall beneath the tower.

In the event building costs escalated and there were insufficient funds to complete the construction work immediately. An additional £30,000 had to be raised to help pay for the new (Western) Infirmary on the adjoining lands of Donaldshill to the west of Gilmorehill. Designed by the Glasgow architect John Burnet in a severe institutional Gothic style for economy, the Western Infirmary was opened in 1874 and completed eight years later. In 1888 Anderson's College of Medicine – by then an independent school with its own teaching staff – was linked to the Western and a handsome building, designed by the Glasgow architect James Sellar with a magnificent sculpture bass relief by Pittendrigh MacGillivray, was constructed for it on Dumbarton Road (pages 20 and 48).

A gift by the Marquess of Bute and an unexpected legacy from Charles Randolph, a former student and later a partner in a leading Clyde shipbuilding and marine engineering firm, made it possible to resume work on the great hall – the Bute Hall – in 1877. Although the plan followed the original outline, Scott prepared new and simpler designs with the advice of the Marquess of Bute, perhaps the greatest architectural patron of the period. The interior was turned round with the focus of the building to the south instead of to the west. A huge gallery across the whole east side was abandoned in favour of a more modest one running round three sides of the main hall. And an ante-chamber, the Randolph Hall, for smaller functions was divided by a screen from the main hall. Scott died in 1878 before construction work began and the building was completed by his son John Oldrid Scott and Edwin Morgan.

The onset in 1878 of the worst recession in

collapse of the City of Glasgow Bank and badly affected the city's construction industry, had, however, prevented any further fund-raising and led to further modifications in the design to reduce costs, including a decision not to proceed with a lead spire on the roof of the Bute Hall in the manner of an Oxford or Cambridge College. The architectural effect of the interior of the Hall is however stunning. Soaring slender cast-iron columns reach to a decorated vaulted roof and from the outside the impression is of pure medieval romanticism with the hall resting on a massive open vaulted stone undercroft. Access was by two grand staircases – the southern leading up to the Senate Room and the northern, the Randolph Staircase, to the central hall of the Hunterian Museum and incorporating a cramped Court Room (now the Robing Room) and the Hunterian Coin Room. Beneath the Randolph Hall was the matriculation office. As soon as the new hall was inaugurated in 1884 it was used for examinations, church services, graduations, and other great occasions. Originally the leaded windows were of clear glass; but these were gradually replaced with stained-glass panels, some in memory of University personalities including Janet Galloway, Secretary of Queen Margaret College (1883–1909).

The spire and four accompanying turrets rising above Gilmorehill – a landmark and

Pearce Lodge composed of the Gatehouse and fragments of the Old College.

symbol of the University – were completed between 1887 and 1891, again by John Oldrid Scott. The original design had been for a ponderous lead-covered clock tower reminiscent of the Cloth Hall at Ypres, but the open lattice stone spire lightened the effect of the whole building. At the same time parts of the Old College, by then completely demolished to make way for the College Goods Station, were brought to Gilmorehill and incorporated in a building designed by A G Thomson, a Glasgow architect, and financed by Sir William Pearce of the Fairfield Shipbuilding and Engineering Company (page 49). Named Pearce Lodge on the north-east side of University Avenue, it was to be used appropriately by the professor of Naval Architecture, whose chair had been newly endowed by Isabella Elder, widow of John Elder, who had originally laid out the Fairfield yard.

Before the move to Gilmorehill more than half the students petitioned the Senate to build a gymnasium beside the recreation ground to the west of the new building. They began raising money for the purpose and, after discussion with Scott, the gymnasium was constructed on the site of the old stable block. Designed by Burnet, it was modelled on the new gymnasium at Exeter College, Oxford, and Mr Maclaren was recruited from Oxford to fit it out. It opened in 1872 and closed only in 1946 when it became the University workshop, leaving both students and staff with no place for formal exercise. The old chapel-like building still survives as workshops behind the Chemistry

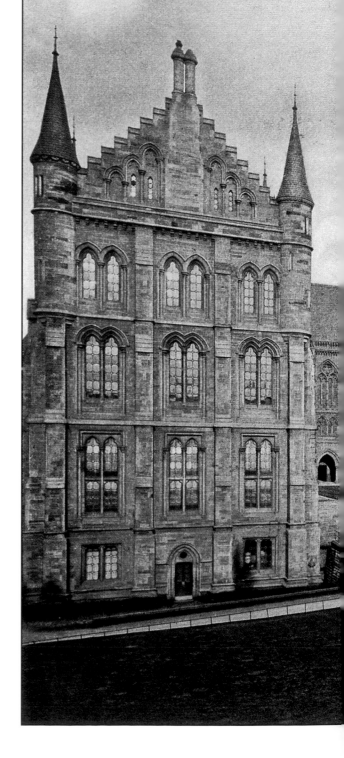

The uncompleted West Quadrangle in about 1892.

Building. Significantly in 1870 there was no provision on Gilmorehill for students to eat, let alone to meet in clubs and societies. The area around the High Street had been thronged with taverns and 'howfs', many with a dubious reputation, but there were few public houses in Byres Road and the University was opposed to any new licences. In 1885 a meeting of students in the Bute Hall resolved to form a University Union – a student club – and raise money for a suitable building on University Avenue alongside the main gate. A donation of £5,000 from Dr John McIntyre, a former student but a graduate of St Andrews, allowed John J Burnet (John's son) to design a building in English collegiate Gothic style. The McIntyre building was completed in 1888 and provided a home for the Union, the newly formed Students' Representative Council (SRC), a meeting place for student clubs and societies and a student restaurant. It was extended to the west in 1893 and again to the south in 1908 and when a new Men's Union was opened at the foot of University Avenue in 1931, the McIntyre building was refurbished for the Queen Margaret Union for women students. And since the building of the new Queen Margaret Union in 1968, it has housed the University bookshop, the Rector's office, and the SRC offices.

By the end of the century changes in teaching methods, greater emphasis on practical laboratory work, and the introduction of new subjects, such as history and political

The opening of the Botany Department in 1900 attended by the most distinguished botanists of the day.

economy, were severely straining the accommodation and new buildings began to be added. This had not been contemplated at the time of the move, when about a third of the site was sold to help create the West End or Kelvingrove Park. In 1900 a Botany building was constructed to the west of the Professors' Square, facing University Avenue, to designs by John Oldrid Scott and John J Burnet. An Engineering laboratory, designed by John J Burnet on the lines of a German technical school, was built in 1901 to the north-east of the main building with funds raised from local industry by the Professor of Civil Engineering, Archibald Barr. And the Anatomy laboratory alongside it was completed three years afterwards.

The main obstacle to further building was shortage of funds and at the time of the Ninth Jubilee celebrations in 1901 Principal Story launched an appeal which over the next five years raised more than £75,000. With additional grants from the newly established Carnegie Trust for the Universities of Scotland, an ambitious new building programme became possible. The first project was the conversion of the Clerk of Senate's office into the Court Room to accommodate the enlarged membership (page 103) and the construction of offices for the Principal and the Clerk of Senate in the Examination Hall on the same floor of the main building. The massive West Medical Building to house Physiology, Materia Medica, Forensic Medicine and Public Health on the sloping ground running down to Dumbarton Road was completed between 1903 and 1907 in an unusual Scots Renaissance style by James Miller after an open competition. The Natural

Philosophy building facing the West Medical Building, by Burnet, was constructed in 1906 under the supervision of Kelvin's successor, Professor Andrew Gray, who had trained as a stonemason in his youth. The space vacated by Natural Philosophy in the main building was taken over by Naval Architecture, whose premises in Pearce Lodge were cramped and uncomfortable. And the Engineering laboratories, which were already too small, were extended in 1908.

By the first decade of the twentieth century the number of arts subjects taught in the University was growing rapidly and the uncompleted Arts West Quadrangle could not provide adequate space for them. Consideration had already been given as to the best way of closing the west side and in desperation the Arts Faculty asked the Court in 1909 urgently to address their needs. A committee, chaired by the new Principal, Sir Donald MacAlister, agreed that priority must be given to completing the west quadrangle, and include a University Chapel that had been discussed for almost twenty years without finding benefactors. By the spring of 1914 John J Burnet had produced a number of schemes and in August he was commissioned to begin work. The outbreak of war that month prevented any further progress until 1919 when it was then decided that the Chapel would be a memorial to the 733 members of the University who had fallen in the conflict. Work began in 1923 but strikes and bad weather delayed completion until early 1929. The effect from outside is dramatic. The Chapel majestically bisects the

The University chapel.

new west facade. The interior is appealingly simple with bold sculptures by Archibald Dawson and fine carved stalls by Walter Gilbert. A series of ten stained-glass windows by the artist Douglas Strachan, funded by graduates, depicting the whole of human life as a spiritual endeavour were installed in 1931. Since then more stained-glass windows have been added. On both sides of the Chapel are teaching and staff rooms for the Arts Faculty, a new Fore Hall – a clumsy pastiche of Scott's architecture – and rooms in the basement for academic and administrative staff to meet – the College Club.

Before work had even started on the Chapel, Burnet had finished two more contracts on Gilmorehill, another extension to Engineering in 1920 and, beside Natural Philosophy, a striking new building for Zoology with a forbidding channelled stone exterior dominated by a classical roof lantern. Some of the new buildings to the west of the University were constructed on the recreation ground and this was replaced by new sports grounds at Bankhead near Scotstounhill in 1906 and Westerlands at Anniesland in 1912. After a public appeal and many fund-raising activities by students (page 75), the Westerlands grounds were extended in the early 1920s and a Pavilion designed by J M Honeyman constructed between 1924 and 1926. In 1996 the University's playing fields with all-weather surfaces were relocated on the Garscube estate, two miles west of Gilmorehill.

The slump in the inter-war years delayed further building. Chemistry was seeking to move from its temporary laboratories opened in 1904 adjoining the 'Abbot's Kitchen' and now in danger of collapse. To illustrate their inadequacy, the Professor of Chemistry arranged for his students to conduct a serious of noxious experiments during a visit by the Rector, Sir Iain Colquhoun, a health fanatic. He intervened with the Principal and work began in 1936 on a large new Chemistry Institute beside Zoology, designed by T Harold Hughes and D S R Waugh in a radical new style. Brick rather than masonry was used and the unashamedly modern exterior of three blocks was linked by slender glazed stairwells. The Professor of Zoology, Edward Hindle, was outraged that the new building would obstruct the view from his office and classroom and to placate him the architects added frivolously a frieze depicting the origin of species facing his building. Completion was interrupted by the Second World War and the Institute was finished only in 1954 by Alexander Wright and Kay to modified designs because of the shortage of materials.

Sir Hector Hetherington became Principal in 1936 and immediately re-established a New Buildings Committee which commissioned the architects Hughes and Waugh to provide a long-term scheme for development to the north of University Avenue in Hillhead. Since the University moved to Gilmorehill this area stretching from Byres Road to Bank Street had been largely built over with a mix of tenement blocks, terrace housing and a few grand villas. Hughes and Waugh's plans included replacing some of these houses with a new library around a quadrangle with a simple clock tower, reminiscent of architecture in other universities at the time. The only part of the scheme to be built was however the innovative and award-winning Round

Reading Room – more elegant in appearance than in utility for its purpose - intended to form the centrepiece of the quadrangle.

Immediately after the war, recognising that Glasgow urgently needed new buildings, the University Grants Committee (UGC), now permitted for the first time to fund capital projects, approved extensions to the Chemistry and Natural Philosophy buildings, and a new Surgery building. The Natural Philosophy Building was by the well-known Edinburgh architect Basil Spence, who was to design several buildings for the University over the next twelve years. A new Veterinary Studies building was constructed in parkland on the Garscube Estate, purchased in 1947. Indeed a completely new campus at Garscube was considered, but the University preferred to extend into Hillhead and the architect Sir Frank Mears was commissioned to draw up a development plan for the area bounded by University Avenue, Byres Road, Great George Street and Hillhead Street. Submitted in 1951, the plan included a new library, an art gallery, a student recreational building, additional teaching facilities and student residences arranged around open quadrangles connected by covered walkways. It entailed the demoli-

tion of a large number of residential properties and the rehousing of the occupants by Glasgow Corporation in new housing schemes. Accepted in principle, it was not followed in detail. Indeed funds did not permit any building on Hillhead for eight years and it was to be another thirty years before his plan can be said to have been implemented even in broad terms.

A Modern Languages Building was constructed in 1958 in University Gardens and the Stevenson Physical Education Building in Oakfield Avenue in 1960. Priority was given to further extensions to Natural Philosophy and Engineering (completed in 1958 and 1959 on the site of the 'Abbot's Kitchen'), an Institute of Virology (1961) adjacent to Anderson's College of Medicine and facing Church Street, a roof laboratory on the Chemistry Building (1963) and a Biochemistry Building adjoining the east side of the West Medical Building (1963). At the same time a Veterinary Hospital was built at Garscube in 1957 to designs by the adventurous and innovative Glasgow architects Gillespie Kidd

---

A model of the proposed development of Hillhead by Sir Frank Mears, 1951.

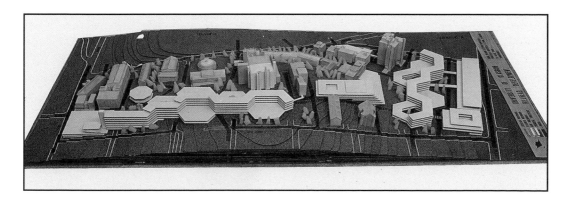

& Coia. Two urgently needed student halls of residence were commissioned to meet the projected growth in numbers in the 1960s – Queen Margaret Hall originally for women in Bellshaugh Road (1964 – extended 1967) and Wolfson Hall at Garscube (1965 – extended 1967). The design of Wolfson Hall with its intriguing skyline by Grenfell Baines and Hargreaves – Building Design Partnership of Preston was the outcome of a closed competition.

The vast increase in student numbers led to rapid building development in Hillhead during the late 1960s. Houses in University Gardens, Lilybank Gardens and Bute Gardens were progressively adapted for use by departments, mostly in the Arts Faculty, and a large student refectory with associated shops (later named the 'Hub') was opened in 1966. A new Queen Margaret Union for women students at the end of University Gardens was completed in 1968 and an extension to the Men's Union was added on the corner of Gibson Street. The Adam Smith Building facing Lilybank House (the original Queen Margaret Hall) for departments in the Social Sciences was completed in 1967 and a Mathematics Building in University Gardens and the Rankine Engineering Building in Oakfield Avenue in 1969. These buildings represent 1960s public architecture at its worst with their bold use of concrete and glass. Phase 1 of the new Library in Hillhead Street, an ambitious design by William Whitfield with tall functional towers piercing the skyline as a modern foil for Scott's Gothic conception, was completed in 1968 (page

The Boyd-Orr Building, 1972.

62). The connected Art Gallery with an austere serrated concrete facade and incorporating a reconstruction of the interior of Rennie Mackintosh's house, demolished to make way for the Refectory, was not finally completed until 1978. The second phase of the Library to modified designs because of cuts in public expenditure was built in 1982–3 and a third in 1986. Kelvin's original classroom in the south front of the West Quadrangle, which survived in its original form, was converted in 1969 into a remarkably unsympathetically designed Senate Room as the original room was now too small for the growing number of professors.

Although many of the University's modern buildings have not stood the test of time, they reflect contemporary design and the ambitious use of non-traditional materials, and nearly all were designed by prominent architects with national reputation for university and other public buildings. The Boyd-Orr Building built in 1972 for basic instruction in science is, apart from the Library, the largest in Hillhead. Designed by Dorward, Matheson, Gleave and Partners of Glasgow it is a massive concrete construction with a copper roof and out of all proportion with its surroundings. The new Geology building of 1980 at the south end of Lilybank Gardens, signalled a return to the use of brick away from the unrelieved drabness of poured concrete. This was followed in 1983 by the Hetherington Building for modern languages in similar style and marked the end of the expansion plan conceived by Frank Mears more than thirty years earlier. Away from the main campus at Garscube a new Veterinary School was built next to the

Hospital between 1969 and 1970, along with the Alexander Stone Building equipped with botanical and microbiological research laboratories and teaching and research blocks were added to the new hospital buildings at Glasgow Royal Infirmary and the Western Infirmary.

By the 1980s public opinion favoured conservation and adaptation of old buildings rather than demolition to make way for new. In Glasgow the destruction of large areas of what many believed to be the finest Victorian city in Britain was decried and in keeping with this change of attitude the University in the 1980s and 1990s has devoted attention to the restoration of its own magnificent architectural heritage. These include houses in Hillhead that were formerly private homes, such as Lilybank House restyled by Alexander (Greek) Thomson in 1863–5 at the end of Lilybank Terrace; the splendid central block in University Gardens (2–10) originally Saughfield Terrace designed by John J Burnet; 12 University Gardens in Art Nouveau style by J Gaff Gillespie; and Burnet's own home with his pavilion drawing office at 80 Oakfield Avenue. The most imaginative refurbishment is the north side of Lilybank Gardens, built between 1880 and 1883, to provide modern accommodation principally for Computing Science. In 1988 the two houses on the south side of Professor's Square were completely renovated in keeping with the original design as a larger Lodging for the Principal and used for entertainment and receptions. The Scott building itself has been progressively restored

Looking north from the University Tower across Hillhead in 1901.

Top: Murano Street Student Village, 1994.
Left: The new Library, 1968.

and redecorated beginning with the Bute Hall, the Hunterian Museum and the Upper Library Hall. The facade of Anderson's College of Medicine, part of the University since 1947 (page 110) has been preserved with a completely new building behind. The materials used in recent buildings such as the 1991 Robertson Building for Biotechnology and Dermatology on the slope of the hill below Zoology are more in keeping with the tradi-

tional architecture on Gilmorehill itself. Away from the campus, Garscube has continued to be developed for Veterinary and Equine Studies, Botany and Oncology. The largest single project in the 1990s has been the construction of the Murano Street Student Village at Ruchill at a cost of £17 million with a mix of accommodation for more than 1,000 students which goes far to answering the University's need for an adequate number of residences for the increasing numbers of students from outside the west of Scotland.

CHAPTER 4

To be a student on Gilmorehill

When the University moved to Gilmorehill there were still no formal entrance qualifications and any form of compulsory entrance examination was strongly resisted. There were, however, voluntary preliminary examinations which could exempt students from first-year classes in some subjects and the bursary competition, with about fifty open awards, which surprisingly did not guarantee a place at the University. Efforts were made at the time of the move to attract new endowments and within ten years the number of bursaries had almost doubled. Although a few students still came to university before they were seventeen, most were older and a good number were in their twenties and early thirties. The majority still came from the west of Scotland – in 1887 nearly seventy per cent had been born in the shires of Lanark, Renfrew, Ayr and Dumbarton. Students continued to come from England, Wales and Ireland, most probably from Presbyterian or free church backgrounds, and some five per cent came

from overseas, particularly India but also north America, Australasia, and even Meiji Japan – often attracted by the fame of Lord Kelvin and Glasgow's growing reputation for engineering and naval architecture. By far the largest number of undergraduates came from professional or middle-class backgrounds – almost thirty per cent had fathers in the church, the law, teaching or finance and accountancy. There were, however, many from less prosperous homes with fathers working in service, in skilled trades, and as farm servants.

Most students lived at home and commuted to the University by train and tram. John Buchan, the statesman and popular novelist, recalled that as a student in the 1890s, he walked from his home in Govan 'through

---

Top: Kaichi Watanabe, a Japanese student, in the centre demonstrating the cantilever principle used in the Forth Bridge, 1890. Bottom: University football team in the 1880s.

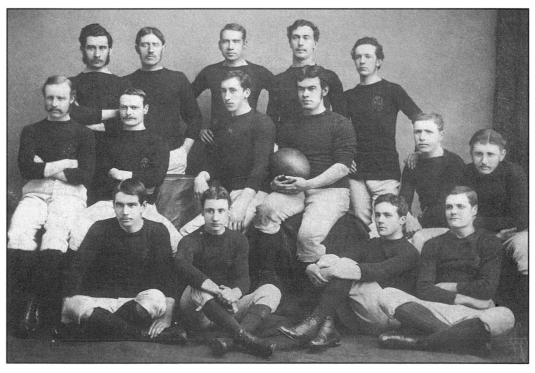

New graduates celebrating their success.

Honorary graduands: Sister Helen Prejean, Hannah Gordon, Sir Peter Maxwell Davies.

Two images of student life, 1891.

every variety of weather with which Glasgow fortifies her children'. Those who came from a distance, if they could afford them, found good lodgings nearby in Partick, Kelvingrove and Woodlands. Others continued to use the old lodging houses in the city centre and the east end where the quality, particularly those taken by poorer students, became a cause of concern. There were reports of harsh landladies who forbade the use of gas lights after eleven at night and of students who could barely afford food. At the time of Rectorial campaigns when students were often canvassed at their lodgings the plight of the less fortunate was all too evident. During the campaign in 1884 when Edward Lushington, Professor of Greek until 1875, was elected,

his supporters were shocked by what they saw – 'dirty unfurnished rooms, the scanty store of books, the pitiably meagre fare'. They appealed for subscriptions from fellow students to establish a Student Medical Aid Society to provide help for the most needy and to discourage those in trouble from suffering in silence. Shortly afterwards lists of lodgings near to the University, with details of facilities and the names of referees, began to be compiled by the students.

The student cut off by poverty from the social life of the university was far removed from the ideal of the undergraduate experience sketched out by Principal Caird in his well received inaugural address in 1874. He challenged students to approach their university studies as 'not technical or profes-

Principal Caird in the pulpit, 1891.

sional' but as providing a 'general or liberal culture' which would enable them to converse with ease on many subjects and in many situations in later life. This entailed not merely attending lectures; but also taking a full part in student activities. The clubs that had been a feature of the Old College migrated to Gilmorehill – the Dialectic Society established in 1862 as a debating society, the Medico-Chirurgical Society founded in 1802, the Theological Society, the University Missionary Society, the Independent Club, the Liberal Association and the Conservative Club. The demands for better recreational and social facilities that resulted in the construction of the gymnasium and later the Union reflected the growing belief that some

form of corporate life for both students and staff was an essential ingredient of a university education. This was accompanied by proposals that all students should once again wear gowns to create a sense of community, and complaints that Glasgow lacked a tradition of student songs for all occasions from graduation ceremonies to lectures were met by the compilation of a student song book. Fund raising for the gymnasium brought students together and provided a focus for all sports under the direction of its first superintendent Mr Maclaren who on his retirement presented the University with the Oxford medal to be awarded annually to the best athlete. At first the only formal sports club was the University Rugby Club set up in 1869 and in 1873 a founder member of the Scottish Football Union. In 1877 an

Association Football Club was formed and the first boat race between Edinburgh and Glasgow Universities took place. Glasgow University Athletic Club was formed in 1881 to promote all kinds of athletic exercise and within ten years it had rugby, tennis, golf, and cricket sections with a large programme of fixtures.

In 1885 the students responded rather belatedly to Principal Caird's vision by organising a well-attended meeting in the newly completed Bute Hall to form a University Union 'for the purpose of promoting social intercourse among the students'. With his support a site on University Avenue was earmarked and the new Union Board began the formidable task of raising the necessary funds and commissioning a suitable building. The meeting to establish the Union also gave birth the following year to the Students Representative Council (SRC) to provide a channel of communication between the growing number of students and the University and 'to promote social and academic unity among the students'. This was assisted by the formation of more student societies reflecting contemporary concerns, for example the Christian Union in 1886 and the Total Abstinence Society in 1889. Others had a subject focus; for example the Alexandrian Society to study the literature of ancient Greece and Rome, and the Philosophical Society – both established in 1887, and the Engineering Society in 1891. Under the 1889 Universities (Scotland) Act Rectors

were required to consult SRCs before nominating their Assessor on University Courts and this slight recognition encouraged the SRCs of all four Scottish universities to persevere with joint meetings to discuss matters of mutual interest including the curriculum and, perhaps more productively, compile the Scottish Universities Student Song Book. Much of the Glasgow SRC's time in its first years was devoted to fund raising for the new Union building and for improved sports facilities, culminating in a great Bazaar at the University in December 1889. Its remarkable success in raising over £14,000, £4,000 more than the original target, was the outcome of the combined efforts of students, graduates, staff and their families and friends. The Union opened in 1890 and soon became the

centre of student life, providing meeting rooms for clubs as well as a debating chamber. Perhaps its most important function was to serve hot lunches and provide a place to smoke and play games of chance – but not to drink. Alcohol could only be brought in for evening dinners if members gave a fortnight's notice. In 1889 the SRC also resolved to begin publishing GUM – The Glasgow University Magazine – monthly during term to keep students informed of progress with the fund-raising and of events. GUM quickly established a reputation for the quality of both its articles and cartoons, attracting contributions from students who were later to become well known in the world of journalism and literature.

Amongst the stallholders at the Bazaar were women from Queen Margaret College, whose students were admitted to the University from 1892 (page 35). Not all male students welcomed the arrival of women and the Union and some societies refused to admit them. The Athletic Club did not establish a Queen Margaret section until 1902 and then mainly for hockey. Queen Margaret College continued to have its own societies including a Christian Union and a Literary and Debating Society which met at the College. Queen Margaret Union had been in existence for some years before a permanent building was acquired in 1908 after a fund-raising campaign had collected £8,000. Recognition of the right of women to higher education was part of much wider changes in social attitudes at the end of the nineteenth century. Much of the rhetoric of self-help and thrift was

Bazaar stewards, 1889.

challenged by socialists and theologians, such as Principal Caird, who emphasised the social message of the gospel. These views found practical expression in 1889 with the establishment of the Glasgow University Students' Settlement Society to provide accommodation for less-well-off students in Garscube Road and undertake social work and educational classes in poorer parts of Glasgow. Queen Margaret College Settlement with a residence in Port Street opened in 1897. New ideas were reflected in clubs such as the Fabian Society, the Socialist Club and the Queen Margaret College Suffrage Society. The most contentious political issue of the period was Irish home rule, supported by the Liberal government from 1905, and Irish National Societies were formed in both the University and Queen Margaret College. There were also occasions for celebration. The students organised week-long events to mark Lord Kelvin's jubilee in the chair of Natural Philosophy in 1896 and played an active part in the week of celebrations for the University's ninth jubilee in 1901.

In 1892 the Scottish universities for the first time introduced formal entrance qualifications, either by passing an entrance exam or by achieving the newly introduced school-leaving certificate. Standards in schools were improving and more students gained the passes necessary to come to university but, despite the increased number of bursaries, many could not afford to do so. In 1901 Andrew Carnegie, a fabulously wealthy Scottish American steel magnate, established a trust with a capital of $10 million to meet

Queen Margaret students, 1891.

O. H. Mavor – James Bridie, the author.

student fees and to assist the Scottish universities more generally. The effect at Glasgow was striking. The number of students rose sharply; men from 1,700 in 1900 to 2,250 in 1913 and women from 350 to 660. Because the grants made no provision for maintenance, the proportion of local students climbed to well over 80 per cent for men and 90 per cent for women. The numbers coming from England and Presbyterian Ireland fell because of much better local provision for university education in both countries, but the number of students born abroad doubled to about ten per cent.

The long depression that hit West of Scotland trade and industry at the beginning of the century fundamentally changed student attitudes. According to contemporaries they lost interest in the Union and clubs and societies, probably because of poverty and greater uncertainty about future employment. The University responded by setting up an Appointments Committee to help graduates find work. Those who remained active in the SRC commented on the lack of corporate life at Gilmorehill and made efforts to encourage participation. O H Mavor, better known as the playwright James Bridie, invented Daft Friday – a celebration of the last day of term – for this very purpose in about 1905. He was one of a glittering band of students at this time whose talent was most evident in GUM, particularly in their delightful pen and ink drawings, and who later achieved fame in many walks of life. The Union building was extended to make more room for meetings and dances and a licence obtained to sell alcoholic drinks on the premises. Funds were also raised for a new sports ground at Anniesland, badly needed because the playing fields at Gilmorehill were being built over. Another feature of the Edwardian age was the growth in the number of Catholic and Jewish students in what had been largely a Presbyterian institution and by the 1910s they had formed their own student associations.

Increasingly tense relations with Germany after 1910 led to the active encouragement of male students to join the newly formed Officers Training Corps (OTC) with places for 400 cadets. Under the command of the bellicose Professor of History, Captain Dudley Medley, the Corps provided basic military training to equip students to volunteer at time of national emergency. When war was declared in 1914 OTC members were amongst the first to be mobilised. Within twelve months over 2,200 members of the University had volunteered and over three hundred students in Arts, Theology and Law were working in munitions factories. The OTC was enlarged and the War Office commandeered lecture rooms to train officers from all parts of the United Kingdom. By the end of the war over 4,400 members of the University, including 1,500 undergradu-

ates, had served and nearly 750 had died. Women also served, some as members of the Scottish Women's Hospital in Serbia and France. The effect on the University was traumatic. Student numbers fell and by 1916 there were almost as many women as men students.

Immediately the war ended in 1918, students flocked back to the University. Numbers recovered to a record 3,000 and reached almost 5,000 by 1921. Although the total slipped back during the 1920s, strikingly the percentage of women rose from about 25 per cent before the war to over 30 per cent. The growth in numbers of women students coupled with the newly won right to vote strengthened the role of the Queen Margaret Union. Since women were still taught in both the College and at Gilmorehill, the Union was the natural focus for social activities. Political debates, similar to those in the Men's Union, began to be held and most students clubs and societies now had some women serving as office bearers. During and immediately after the war several new student clubs were formed, for example the Alchemists Club (1916), the Chess Club (1919), the Critic Club – the successor of the Fabian Club (1921), the Middle Class Club (1919) and a branch of the Alliance Club with the object of promoting 'Purity in our National life' was begun with Professor Glaister as its President. In the inter-war years the complexion of Scottish politics changed with a revival in calls for some measure of self-government and in 1927 a student Scottish Nationalist Association was formed.

The experience of the war had led many Scotsmen to believe that the English tradition of sports and social activities as an integral part of education had much to recommend it. With the encouragement of the Principal, Sir Donald MacAlister, the Student Welfare Scheme was conceived in 1921 to raise £150,000 to re-invigorate student life by funding an extension to the Men's Union (in fact a new building), improved sports facilities – notably a pavilion, and student halls of residence. Although some large donations were received, the bulk of the funds were raised by the students themselves. Another enormous bazaar with numerous side shows and attractions at Gilmorehill in November 1923 brought in over £20,000. Running costs of the new facilities were to be met from a Student Fund set up in 1929 when a compulsory annual fee paid by all students was introduced in all Scottish universities. More certain and regular funding made it possible for the Athletic Club to support a greater range of sports and to compete over a larger area. In 1926–7 the Football Club was the first university side to win the Scottish Amateur Cup. Students were not concerned only to raise money for themselves. For example an annual Charities Day was inaugurated in 1921 for the Lord Provost's welfare fund and for more than fifty years was a great event in the Glasgow calendar.

Glasgow University OTC at camp, 1914.

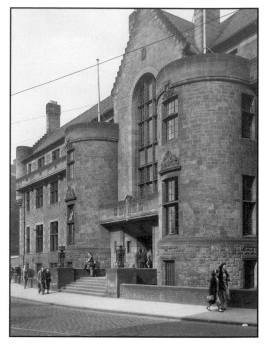

The new Men's Union was opened in 1931 by the Rector, the author Compton Mackenzie, and the existing Union, the Macintyre building, was given over to the Queen Margaret Union. Despite the better building and larger debating chambers, students remained curiously uninterested in political events in Europe until the eve of war. There were occasional peace and disarmament meetings but no serious protest until 1937 when Canon Dick Sheppard, a leading member of the Peace Pledge Union, was elected Rector. These were years of world-wide economic slump and the students were more concerned to relieve the suffering of the unemployed in their local communities on Clydeside. With their help the Queen Margaret Settlement based in Anderston, one of the most depressed areas, set up clubs for out-of-work men and women and a nursery school. This voluntary effort was sustained by the Charities day with its now familiar slogan 'and a Penny', which was raising £10–£15,000 a year for City charities. The economic and social problems of the region were of special concern to the growing body of students with nationalist sympathies, who believed that if the smaller nations of eastern Europe could be granted independence so could Scotland.

The world depression, symbolised by the unfinished hull of Ship Number 534, later the liner Queen Mary, at Clydebank, brought financial difficulties to many West of Scotland families, even those in the middle class, making university education difficult to afford.

Top left: The circular for the Grand Bazaar, 1923.
Top right: Glasgow University Union in 1950.
Bottom: Students on Charities Day in the 1930s.

There was also little incentive for young people to further their studies. There were few jobs for graduates, particularly in teaching. Glasgow student numbers, which reached a peak of almost 5,600 in 1931, fell away steadily to less than 4,300 by the outbreak of Second World War in 1939, with a greater decline in the number of women students – from nearly 1,700 to just over 1,100. And the resulting drop in fee income placed great strain on the University's fragile finances (page 98).

Student sympathy with pacifism was short-lived. In the aftermath of the Munich crisis in 1938, the Union voted to impeach Neville Chamberlain for his policy of appeasement. When war was declared in September 1939 conscription was introduced immediately; but the government recognised that science had an important part to play in securing victory and that educated men and women would be essential in rebuilding the country when peace came. Efforts were made to ensure that qualified men could attend universities for two terms before being called up and that those studying medicine, engineering and some sciences could complete their degrees in accelerated programmes. The number of male students in Glasgow, therefore, did not decline as sharply as in the First World War and there was only a modest rise in the number of women, who were also required to serve in the forces or in war work. As before all students were regarded as potential officers. Training was provided by the OTC, the University Air Squadron – in January 1941 the first to be formed in any university – and a Naval Division, set up in 1942. The University tower was a prominent

77

landmark for enemy aircraft and a volunteer fire service of staff and students was set up in November 1940 to safeguard the building. In the event only one bomb landed near to the University – in Kelvin Way in the spring of 1942, breaking most of the windows in the south front of the building, but not preventing exams taking place the following day, the students crunching their way across the glass-strewn floors to their tables in the Bute Hall. Throughout the war the Principal Sir Hector Hetherington wrote an open letter every year to students, staff and graduates on active service to let them know of his concern for them and tell them something of life at the University. Altogether 432 members of the University gave their lives during the Second World War and their names were added to the memorial in the University chapel.

In 1945 demobilised servicemen began to flood back to the University as part of the post-war educational programme and within four years the number of men had climbed to a record 6,000. There were enormous strains on facilities but not the same atmosphere of rowdiness and misbehaviour in these early days of peace that characterised many universities. There was, however, a strong commitment to Scottish nationalism amongst the students. Sir Archibald Sinclair, Rector from 1938 to 1945, supported some measure of Home Rule for Scotland and in 1950 John MacCormick, author of the New Scottish Covenant, was elected Rector. During that year Glasgow Nationalist students, to the fury of the Principal, audaciously removed the Stone of Destiny taken to England by Edward I in 1296 from Westminster Abbey and returned it to Scotland.

Student television in the 1990s.

There had been concern since at least the 1920s about the many students who took little or no part in the corporate life of the university – as much a reflection of the high proportion of students who lived at home as any lack of opportunity to join student societies at Gilmorehill. This became an important issue in the 1950s as the University Grants Committee (UGC) began to place emphasis on corporate life in the student experience. In his addresses to first-year students the Principal repeatedly encouraged students to participate in sports and social activities; but to little effect. For many unfairly dubbed 'brownbaggers', it was simply impossible. Home was often over an hour away and grants, which were lower than those in England, only covered the minimum living expenses. The University did not attract more students from further afield; in part

because it lacked sufficient halls of residence. And when students did participate actively at Rectorial elections, the publicity was not always welcome. The fight – a battle of the gates – for possession of the door into the east quadrangle on the south front was abandoned in 1953 after two students were injured and the boisterous installation of the Home Secretary R A Butler as Rector in 1956 caused an outcry in the press and brought to an end the old hustings-style elections and triumphal addresses.

Throughout the 1950s the University attempted to restrain student numbers, partly to prevent a decline in standards and partly until sufficient new buildings had been provided, in particular a new library, gymnasium, and a better students' canteen. As a result the post-war peak of 7,500 was not reached again until 1962. Then in the wake

A seminar in the 1990s.

of the Robbins Report on Higher Education and the introduction of universal student grants, the student population began to rise steadily. Glasgow did not witness the student disturbances that occurred in many other British universities during the late 1960s, although there were pressures for student representation on the Senate and Court. There was also a spectacular confrontation between the students and the University in 1965 when a group of students were accused of making obscene telephone calls to the female Clerk of SRC. The University handled the case badly and was forced not only to retreat but to review the whole procedure for handling disciplinary cases. The incident was deeply damaging to relations with students and the wider community in Glasgow, which largely sided with the students.

By the 1960s the mood of the students was beginning to change towards greater social concern as it had done in the 1930s. At first they identified with the opponents of the apartheid regime in South Africa electing Chief Luthuli and Winnie Mandela as Rectors; then they became concerned about the profound problems of the local economy which was in the grip of massive structural changes. In 1971 the students expressed their solidarity with the work-in at the collapsed Upper Clyde Shipbuilders by electing a leader of the shop stewards Jimmy Reid as Rector. Even when Glasgow elected a student rector in 1978 they chose John Bell, a radical theology student in the tradition of Dick Sheppard. Significantly since then Rectors have increasingly been popular media figures, albeit at times with clear agendas either for political change or improved student welfare.

During much of the 1960s and 1970s the main pre-occupation of student politics was the issues of compulsory membership and of 'mixing' of the two unions. Successive governments were unwilling to make funds available for badly needed new student facilities unless both conditions were met and the Men's Union remained firmly opposed to such reforms, flagrantly flaunting its male interests and disregarding female feelings by putting on strip shows. This enraged feminists, who aggressively picketed the Union. It was not until 1980 that mixed unions were accepted. A little earlier students along with lecturers had gained the right to elect representatives on the University's govern-

Pranks during the Rectorial address, 1950.

ing bodies. The Union has a tradition, which still continues, for the quality of its orators, winning successive national and international debating competitions.

By the time the decision to mix the unions was taken, the proportion of women students at Glasgow was over 40 per cent and by 1995 half the full-time students were women. At the same time the proportion of students living at home has fallen. There were now two universities in Glasgow, and west of Scotland students more often chose to leave home to study in other Scottish universities. And very many more students from England, first predominantly from the north, then from all counties, and many from Northern Ireland, came to Glasgow. The University remains essentially Scottish but 17 per cent of students come from elsewhere in the United Kingdom and 13.5 per cent from outside it. Student concerns, not only at Glasgow, have recently of necessity become more personal as grants have been reduced and students loans introduced. Many students again find it hard to make ends meet and are worried about repaying loans when jobs are hard to find, reinforcing the need to complete courses on time. Gone are the days when a few students could take a leisurely path to a degree, devoting most of their time to student politics and societies. Nevertheless for all students there are more opportunities than ever before to participate in sport and in clubs and societies. Glasgow's enviable reputation for debating continues and students trained at the University represent their countries in events throughout the world.

CHAPTER 5

Teaching and learning

The move to Gilmorehill did not bring an immediate change in teaching. The new buildings provided better but not different facilities; the curriculum was unchanged; and teaching continued to be almost entirely by lecture – five a week in degree classes. Students in Latin and Greek translated and commented in class and for some years the philosophy classes continued to meet to examine students and hear essays read. Attendance at laboratories was largely voluntary but medical students received bedside instruction in the wards and practised dissection as they had done since the eighteenth century. Almost all lectures were given by the professors, most conscientious and some inspirational teachers. For example, William Thomson, Lord Kelvin, Glasgow's most eminent nineteenth-century scientist, professor of Natural Philosophy from 1846 until 1899, demonstrated on the bench with the help of an assistant, questioned and spoke with his students, explained his current experiments and encouraged

them to assist with them. There were a small number of untenured assistants in subjects such as Latin and Greek with large numbers of students and several classes and the number of lecturers in specialised fields of medicine did increase. But it was only after 1900 that many lecturers began to be appointed to teach new subjects or reinforce professorial departments, and the authority of the professor in his department remained largely unquestioned until the 1960s.

Radical change in the curriculum came in 1893. The old progression of degree subjects in Arts ended and a Science Faculty and the first full Science degree were created. The range of subjects and classes then slowly increased and by 1939 there were more than 120 non-clinical lecturers. Teaching methods were however slow to change because funds were always limited but from 1901 dedicated buildings with better facilities began to be built for some science, medical and engineering departments. Arts had to wait until

1929 when the War Memorial Chapel and a significantly different range of rooms for teaching were built to complete the west side of the 1870 building. There was a hall with an ancient name, the Fore Hall, six modest lecture rooms and thirty-one small staff rooms used for teaching. Major change came with increased government funding in the 1950s and 1960s which permitted more staff, new subjects and classes and more personal teaching. Lectures, by teams of lecturers rather than the professor alone, remained the normal method of teaching the large first- and second-year classes, but there were many more advanced classes, individual tutorials, seminars, printed bibliographies and hand-outs, more sophisticated laboratory work and, later, extensive computing facilities.

Increasing numbers of students specialised. A majority of graduates in Science received Honours degrees from the 1950s; in Arts only from 1981; and to-day the great majority of students in Arts, Science and Social Sciences gain Honours degrees and are taught in their honours years in the same manner as in other British universities.

Until 1893 the Ordinary M.A. remained a four-year degree with a fixed order of subjects – two years of Latin, Greek and Mathematics, better-prepared students exempted from the first year; then Logic and Moral Philosophy, English Literature added in 1859 by University Commissioners, and Natural Philosophy. By

Lord Kelvin's last lecture in 1899.

the 1880s however there were strong advocates for reform. The University Commissioners proposed that the degree should provide 'a tolerably free choice of subjects along certain distinct lines of study adapted to various bents of mind' and in 1892 they legislated for the four Scottish universities. There was to be an entrance or 'preliminary' examination of the type Glasgow had pioneered ten years before. A new three-year M.A. Ordinary degree still required seven passes, all in first-year Ordinary classes, but with choice – Latin or Greek, Logic or Moral Philosophy, Mathematics or Natural Philosophy; a further subject from these six or Chemistry; English or History or a Modern Language; and two more courses. There were already advanced classes in some subjects and most soon offered second-year, Higher Ordinary classes. From 1908, one or two of the seven degree passes had to be in these Higher Ordinary classes and the academic year was extended to twenty-five weeks in three terms. There had been radical change. Students had now to meet entrance standards and many came hoping to graduate and make a career, often in teaching. The regulations have been amended in detail a number of times but the old philosophy endured. Seven passes are still required for the Ordinary M.A. – one from at least three of four subject groups – language, philosophy, mathematics and a fourth group of the remaining subjects in the Faculty, and at least two subjects must be studied for a second year in Higher Ordinary classes.* In the last thirty years more specialised third-year, Advanced Ordinary, classes have come to be offered in most subjects and the range of subjects required for graduation

has been reduced to four. With a normal load of three classes a year students are able to build a general or more specialised Ordinary degree, perhaps with an eye to a career; for example beginning a new language or studying computing or management. A major shift in student choice however began in the 1960s. More and more opted for Honours degrees and in 1995 79 per cent of 730 students graduating M.A. in Arts and almost 72 per cent of 284 graduating in Social Sciences received Honours degrees.

There had been Honours M.A. degrees since 1826 but they required passes in all the traditional subjects and in only a further course in one or more. Although the Royal Commission on Scottish Universities of 1876 wished to introduce single honours degrees on the Oxford model where students concentrated on one subject for their whole period of study, this was resisted and the regulations were only modified in 1893, then radically restructured in 1907. Honours students were required to achieve six passes in their first two years – normally in Ordinary and Higher classes in two prospective Honours subjects and in two other Ordinary classes. They could then complete an Ordinary degree or attend Honours classes and sit 'finals' for an Honours degree in two subjects. At first Honours could be gained in three years but four years soon became normal though obligatory only in 1975. The range of Honours subjects and classes, limited at first, grew and from the 1960s teaching became increasingly specialised and less formal. The 'Scottish' Honours degree however remains 'different' in principle. Students do not

---

*This is the position in 1996 but new regulations for the M.A. Ordinary in Arts are likely to apply to students entering in 1997 (page 91).

specialise immediately. They must study in breadth as well as depth. They may change direction, and about a third do so. The 'difference' arose because the Honours degree grew from the old Ordinary degree with its spread of subjects and because Scottish students came, and still come, younger and with less specialised school qualifications than students from, say, England. Scots consider it an advantage to have this flexibility and it is striking that most of the many students from outside Scotland now coming to study in Glasgow feel the same, even at the cost of an extra year of study.

The range of subjects in Arts soon began to increase. Chairs were founded in History in 1893 and Political Economy in 1896. There were already non-graduating language classes and in 1895 a lectureship in French was created. Lectureships in German and Italian followed in 1899 and 1902, and by 1924 chairs in all three languages and in Spanish had been created – all by endowment. To-day fourteen languages are offered – to beginners if necessary with the support of a Language Laboratory. By 1939 twenty Ordinary classes in Arts and nine in Science could be taken as part of the degree and there were thirteen professors, forty-seven lecturers and twelve assistants in Arts subjects. Staff and subjects increased after 1945, then more sharply in the 1960s. To-day, despite the economies of the 1980s, there are twenty-nine professors and 147 readers and lecturers in Arts and more than sixty subjects in Arts, Divinity, Law, Science and Social Sciences may be studied as part of an Arts degree.
In 1977 a number of Arts departments, head-

ed by Economic History, Political Economy, Politics, Psychology and Sociology, were permitted to constitute a new Faculty of Social Sciences offering Ordinary and Honours degrees of M.A. (Social Sciences) with degree regulations broadly similar to those in Arts. This enabled students to specialise in these disciplines, study subjects from Arts and other faculties and take joint Honours degrees across the faculties. And, if experience leads to a change of mind, it is normally possible for the student to transfer without difficulty from one faculty to the other.

Theology, since 1939 re-named Divinity and a 'higher' Faculty from 1451, has changed greatly since 1945. For centuries most of its students had studied Arts and were preparing to be ministers of the Church. Now the majority are school-leavers or mature students with an interest in religion and theology but not necessarily preparing for the ministry. It is a small faculty of between 150 and 200 students taught in the same ways as in Arts.

The newly-created Faculty of Science of 1893 consisted of the professors of Mathematics, Natural Philosophy, Astronomy, Civil Engineering and Mechanics, and Naval Architecture previously in Arts and the professors of Chemistry, Natural History (Zoology and Geology), Botany, Anatomy and Physiology previously in Medicine. There had been a curious B.Sc. degree since 1873 – in Law, Biological Science, Geological Science or Engineering Science. It required seven or eight passes but the number had to be made up with Arts courses – five in the Law degree, four in Biological Science. Now a full three-year B.Sc. degree in Pure

Science, more specialised than the M.A., was created. It required passes in a first examination in Natural Philosophy, Chemistry, and Mathematics or Biology (Zoology and Botany) and in a Final Examination on a higher standard in three or more Science subjects other than Engineering. The intention was a degree more demanding and 'as nearly as possible equivalent to that of the examination for the degree of Master of Arts with Honours' but by 1921 experience had shown the Arts model was better and a five-subject B.Sc. Ordinary degree with at least two subjects studied for two years and an Honours B.Sc. degree with at least four different subjects studied in the first two years were introduced. The degrees, modified in detail in the 1960s, are now offered on a course-unit basis with a much expanded range and number of subjects including many from other faculties. A majority of Science students began to take Honours degrees in the 1950s and in 1995 over 80 per cent did so. The range of Honours subjects has also expanded – from sixteen in 1960 to forty-three in 1996. The early years are unspecialised as in Arts, and with the same advantages. For example students with an interest in the Biological Sciences may study Chemistry, Biology and another subject in the first year. They may take a more basic class in a subject not studied fully at school. They then decide over two years in which of the many aspects of Biology to specialise – or change direction entirely.

Teaching in Science changed earlier and more radically than in Arts. Until the 1940s, at least in the larger classes, it was chiefly by dictated notes or blackboard work. Laboratory classes had become compulsory early in the

century and facilities were better though the experiments were often routine. Major change came quickly after 1945 because war-time advances had revolutionised some branches of science. 'Big' science, requiring new and expensive facilities, special funding and national planning, came to all universities. Atomic physics in Natural Philosophy is a prime example in Glasgow (page 100). The content and manner of teaching changed and new and more sophisticated laboratory facilities were built. There were many more staff for teaching and funded research. An

increasing number of students took Honours degrees and many went on to research degrees and careers in science outside school-teaching. Postgraduates worked as demonstrators and with members of research teams brought new science and enthusiasm to laboratory classes. For example it became common for students to undertake a research project as a component of their Honours degree, often as part of the department's own research programme.

The four other faculties prepare students for

Students and staff of the Engineering Faculty, 1936.

professional careers and their curricula and teaching must meet the requirements of professional bodies. There has been a large Medical faculty since the late eighteenth century (page 22) and since 1948 it has included Dentistry, previously taught in the Glasgow Dental College, and since 1977 a department and degree course in Nursing Studies. Veterinary Medicine, previously taught in the Glasgow Veterinary College, became a university discipline in 1949 in the Medical Faculty and since 1966 has been a separate Faculty. Law, taught since 1451 and a faculty teaching Scots Law since the eighteenth century (pages 22–4), now incorporates Accountancy, an example of a profession gradually becoming university-trained. Accountants used to qualify by apprenticeship and examination by their professional Institute. The link with the University began in 1925 when a part-time chair of Accountancy was endowed in the Law Faculty offering a class open to law students but taken mainly by accountancy apprentices. In 1956 the Institute required apprentices to spend a year at university taking courses in law and economics. In 1967 the Bachelor of Accountancy degree became the normal entry to the profession in Scotland and in recognition in 1984 the Faculty was re-named Law and Financial Studies with two Schools, Law and Accountancy.

Engineering has been taught in the University since 1840, first in the Faculty of Arts, from 1893 in Science and in 1923, after an unduly long apprenticeship, in its own faculty. It has now five major branches, Civil, Electronics and Electrical, Mechanical, Aerospace, Naval Architecture and Ocean

Engineering, with ever-growing sophistication in teaching and research. It has moved from its old heavy-industry image to advanced electronics and facilities such as the ship-model test tank, the largest in Europe, and the stress-testing equipment and wind tunnel in the Research Services Unit at Spencer Street. And in the last decade it has introduced unusual but successful degree courses in Electronics with Music, in Product Design Engineering taught with Glasgow School of Art and in Technological Education taught with St Andrew's College of Education to train school teachers of modern technology.

Teaching in the professional faculties has changed in much the same manner and time-scale as in the other faculties. There are fewer foundation and more professionally-related courses and a greater range of specialisms; fewer formal lectures; more group teaching, greater use of technology and many discrete initiatives. The Medical, Dental and Veterinary Medicine courses have become increasingly science-based and after two years, three in Veterinary Medicine, taught largely in the University, the best students may complete an 'intercalated' B.Sc. degree before proceeding to the clinical years. Recently there has been positive emphasis on the human aspect of medicine – for example each student is introduced to a local family and follows its social and medical history throughout the course. And a radical new learning programme is about to be introduced (page 92). In Law the basic professional content remains but there are new specialisms and teaching facilities. Technology permits cases and statutes to be consulted on computer; there is an endowed Moot Court Room for

court training; and European languages may be studied as part of the degree or improved in the University Language Centre. European Community Law and national laws are studied and experienced by periods in Brussels and in European universities.

Students in the new buildings at Gilmorehill in 1870 would be astonished by the University of to-day – its size, the content of courses, the personal character of teaching and the range of academic and social facilities. In 1870 the majority must have found it hard travelling across the city, often walking, five days a week, in the winter dark during the single term from November until April. Lectures began at 8 a.m. in gas-lit rooms – electric lighting was introduced to the University in the 1890s by Lord Kelvin. The 'hurry' bell rang (and still rings) until five minutes past the hour while students crowded on the benches with their coats and bags. Attendance was checked by roll-call or assigning seats at the first meeting and having the student at the end of each bench record absentees. The professor entered in his gown and lectured for fifty minutes. Latecomers, if they were permitted to enter, were 'stamped' and the professor might receive the same treatment if he over-ran because students often had a lecture at the next hour and the narrow staircases and quadrangles were crowded with students moving from one class to another. Almost all classes met in the morning – fortunately because facilities for students were minimal. The Men's Union was opened in 1885 but many could not afford to use it. Professors, some meeting several classes during the morning, had the advantage of living in the Professors Court or at least nearby and could return home to breakfast after an early lecture. Lectures were heavily factual and avidly copied by the students for 'good' notes were the basis of most examination answers. Some professors were entirely formal in their lectures, others tried to gauge the understanding of their students and respond to it but tutorial teaching hardly existed. The first professor of History in 1893 was considered a 'manly' figure at his lectern but he rarely met a student. After the turn of the century teaching became more personal. The second professor of History appointed in 1899 made a point of calling out students after his lectures to speak to them individually and sponsored a departmental student society for social purposes. Essays and examinations, some marked outside the University, were normally returned by the 'pigeon-holes' in the classroom with the briefest of comments. The growing number of lecturers – in History one in 1902, three by 1912, and the smaller Higher Ordinary and particularly Honours classes led to brief tutorials and more contact between staff and students. Laboratories gave a limited opportunity for questions. And the growing number of departmental student societies, often well-supported by staff, permitted more informal but often nervous meetings. The conventions of the time and the limited resources of many students certainly made the University distinctly impersonal, but for most it was a serious but not a sad place. Student magazines were bold and enthusiastic, behaviour was at times boisterous, but without maintenance grants, life and pleasures for most students had to be simple and economical.

After 1950 many more members of staff were appointed, first in Science and more generally from the 1960s. Teaching began to be more personal. The large first- and second-year classes changed more slowly but even they become less formal. On the Arts side individual tutorials on written work and, later, seminar groups became ubiquitous. Many more small specialised Honours classes were offered and communication between teachers and students became more frequent and increasingly informal. The old formal 'Sir' address to staff and 'Mr Smith' address to students became unusual. There were better printed and visual materials, more equipment and, more recently, computing has offered new learning techniques and data-handling facilities. The combination of greater numbers of students and reduced state funding since the early 1980s has certainly imposed restrictions on the amount of personal attention given to students but teaching to-day is a world away from what was normal only half a century ago.

There has been another body of students, many of whom never entered the University buildings. Until quite recently Glasgow was a heavily west of Scotland university and since the eighteenth century its mission was not confined to the campus and its matriculated students. A good number of the 'private' students in the eighteenth and nineteenth centuries who paid fees to attend College lectures were mature local men seeking to improve themselves or obtain technical information. And since the move to Gilmorehill courses have been offered specifically for external students. In the 1880s and 1890s a formal programme of 'extension' courses 'of a university character'

The Moot Court Room.

was organised in four centres in Glasgow and fifteen others as distant as Dumfries and Galloway and certificates were offered to those who passed examinations. It was a success for some years and then fell away. In the 1920s members of the University became strongly associated with the Workers Education movement; an Extra-Mural Education Committee was set-up; and funds provided for classes held outside the University, particularly those for working men and during the industrial depression. They were a modest success and when local authority money became available after 1945

the University was quick to expand the work. The first Extra-Mural tutor and in 1947 the first Director of Extra-Mural Studies were appointed and since then external teaching has grown and changed to meet new needs. To-day there is a Department of Adult and Continuing Education serving the University's traditional territory, the Glasgow region and the south and west. There are short courses in academic subjects taken largely by mature students and, more recently, a growing number of courses leading to the award of certificates, for example in Environmental Science and Language Studies. There are courses offering credits which can lead to entry to higher education and certificate and degree courses in Community Education and Development. The University also offers services to school pupils. For some years there has been a very successful annual nine-week Summer School in the University for 250 pupils from priority areas in the Region, assisting them gain admission to college or university and preparing them to study there. Departments also provide services directly for school pupils. For example History and Archaeology have for many years mounted an annual teaching day for sixth-form pupils preparing for advanced examinations and up to six hundred students from Shetland to Galloway, two-thirds of the candidates, have travelled to Glasgow to attend.

The character of teaching and the regulations for degrees have changed in detail over the last century but a basic continuity has been maintained. During the last fifteen years however there have been widespread changes in the terminology of classes and degrees and to an extent in teaching. They have been heady but difficult years for all universities. Government became more interventionist; direct funding was reduced and until recently universities were encouraged to compensate by increasing student numbers. Teaching and research became subject to regular external evaluation with financial rewards and penalties. In Glasgow student numbers grew rapidly and new classes and specialisms were created. Teaching became more sophisticated and specialised – the classic example is the use of the computer as a teaching tool and a resource in the hands of the student. A new generation of university teachers was more willing to see change and

greater flexibility in the old structures. The three 'Scottish' teaching terms, Martinmas, Candlemas and Whitsun, were retained but half-courses and modules were introduced. The Science Faculty began to assign 'course units' to classes in the 1970s – for example a pass in an Ordinary Class counted 20 units, a Higher Ordinary Class 40 units, and a minimum of 160 units was required for the Ordinary B.Sc. Degree. In the 1980s Science replaced the old class designations by 'levels' – for example an Ordinary class became a 'level 1 class', a Higher Ordinary class a 'level 2 class' – but the 'Ordinary' B.Sc. degree still remains. Other faculties, including Divinity, followed Science's example but Arts and Social Sciences did not. Now both will introduce even more radical changes in 1997. 'Ordinary' has become a devalued word with pejorative significance and the Ordinary M.A. in Arts will be replaced by eight subject-designated 'general Humanities' M.A. degrees – for example M.A. (Historical Studies), (Linguistic Studies) or (Literary Studies). Teaching will normally be in half-year modules but there may be half modules or two linked modules. Sixteen modules must be taken to obtain the degree, at least half in core subjects in the area of study, and include a philosophy module and, in some cases, a language module. Performance in each module – with less weight given to written examinations – will be assessed, grade points awarded and the degree may be gained with 'Merit' or 'Distinction'. The smaller Social Sciences Faculty will have only one general degree, an M.A. (Applied Social Science), but a course in research techniques will be compulsory to better prepare graduates for the work-place. The

Honours M.A. in both faculties will be little changed but half-year modules are beginning to replace year-long courses. Breadth and since 1893 choice has been at the heart of the M.A. and these changes are new applications of old principles. There is still freedom to change direction of study and take either a General or an Honours degree but it remains to be seen if the new General discipline-oriented degrees will reverse the trend in student choice to specialised four-year Honours degrees.

The most positive gain in recent years is probably greater flexibility. Diverse entry qualifications are now accepted and there are many mature students There are 'beginners' classes in Introductory Mathematics and General Chemistry and in modern languages. These count as Level l classes and a student who takes one may go on to take an Honours degree. There are fewer lectures and more self-instruction techniques though financial stringency has recently reduced the level of personal attention given to students. Continuous assessment, shorter written degree examinations and exemption from all or part of first- and second-year examinations have become normal. And an increasing number of Glasgow students spend a year of their degree course in European or American universities and a greater number of European and north American students spend a semester or year abroad in Glasgow – to the great academic benefit of Glasgow.

The most sweeping change of all is about to begin in the Medical Faculty. It is accepted that the medical curriculum has become overcrowded with too much emphasis on learning factual information and radical change was recommended by the General Medical Council. In Glasgow the divide between the pre-clinical and clinical phases of medical education will begin to disappear in 1996 and there will be emphasis on 'student-centred' and 'problem-based' learning with teachers becoming much more 'facilitators'. There will be far fewer lectures and laboratories and greater emphasis on students working together in groups to consider cases and learn to define and solve problems. For example the first assignment to a group of first-year students might be to pursue the medical consequences of a road-accident. There will be earlier contact with patients, but less of it in the wards and more in general-practice surgeries, clinics and in the community. This is the early stages of radical change and a Medical Education Unit has been set up in Glasgow to manage and assess the development.

No other faculty has proposed such radical change but every faculty has reviewed its curriculum and teaching in the last two decades. There is greater flexibility and wider student choice though as student numbers increased and funding decreased, one-to-one teaching has been reduced. Group learning and investigation is however more common. It is fair to say that the degrees reformed in the 1890s have permitted flexibility, choice of subjects, the opportunity of either a General or an Honours degrees, and allowed the University great freedom to adapt as scholarship, teaching methods and funding have changed.

CHAPTER 6

Gilmorehill and the Enquiring Mind

It was about the time that the University moved to Gilmorehill that the United Kingdom began to accept the concept, borrowed from Germany, that a university should have two related functions – teaching and research. Fundamental to this view was that research would inform teaching in honours schools being introduced in universities throughout the world. This did not sit easily with the Scottish Ordinary degree, designed to give students a wide range of knowledge that would equip them to be good citizens and in particular to teach in schools. Moreover, while in the German model the professor was the leader of a research team and a civil servant paid directly by the state, in Scotland he was first and foremost a teacher, often with large unruly classes and dependent for most of his income on class fees. In the nineteenth century there was, however, one important attraction of a chair in Glasgow for those who wished to research – the academic year ran only from late October to early April. This is why the famous botanist William

Hooker remained a professor at Glasgow from 1820 to 1841 before becoming Director of the Royal Botanic Gardens at Kew. William Thomson, Lord Kelvin, one of the greatest scientists of his day who held the chair of Natural Philosophy from 1846 to 1899, used the long vacations for research, the practical application of his inventions and extensive travel to meet scientists working in his field. William Macquorn Rankine, the progenitor of modern thermodynamics and professor of Civil Engineering from 1855 to 1873, spent his vacations working with Clyde shipbuilders and engineers helping to pioneer new developments that were to conquer international markets.

The same was not true of medicine where chairs were part-time and much of a clinical professor's time was taken up with hospital duties, provided free of charge, and his own private practice. Joseph Lister, the pioneer of antiseptic surgery and professor of Surgery from 1860 to 1869, was an exception; he left to go to Edinburgh which he judged to be more conducive to research (page 22). In the humanities at the time of the move to Gilmorehill there were a few scholars with national reputations; notably the professor of Moral Philosophy, Edward Caird, later to be Master of Balliol College, Oxford, and his elder brother John, professor of Divinity, considered to be one of the finest preachers of late Victorian Britain. Two great scholars in the humanities who took chairs, Richard Jebb and Gilbert Murray in Greek, used Glasgow as a stepping stone back to chairs at Cambridge and Oxford. The majority of professors were however teachers and most had themselves been educated at Glasgow. The new building on Gilmorehill was demonstrably designed for teaching. There were no research laboratories and since 1826 the library had not enjoyed the copyright privileges to be found in Edinburgh, London, Oxford and Cambridge.

The 1889 Universities (Scotland) Act broke the link between professors' income and class fees; but there was still no imperative for staff to engage in research except for their own interest, though more chose to do so. The new Honours classes made little difference at first; they were effectively additional to Ordinary classes and included little in-depth study. In some new subjects such as English, German, and History good scholars, such as Walter Raleigh, Hermann Fielder and Richard Lodge, came and went, defeated by the teaching load, the weather, and lack of resource. Some men of distinction stayed and made notable contributions to their subjects. Sir Henry Jones, professor of Moral Philosophy from 1894 to 1922, was the lead-

ing British idealist of his generation, attracting research students and helping to shape educational policy in Scotland and his native Wales. William Smart, the first professor of Political Economy (1896–1915), one of the most innovative economists of the time, contributed to the reform of the poor law. Macneile Dixon, professor of English from 1904–35, was both a gifted teacher and an industrious and popular author. These men were hardly typical; most professors in the humanities continued to devote their time to teaching and to University administration.

In science and engineering the research environment, which had declined at the end of Kelvin's long career, improved in the early 1890s with the appointment of three men with different interests, who were committed to laboratory teaching and new scientific research. Frederick Bower came to the chair of Botany in 1885 with experience of the 'new botany' being taught in London; Archibald Barr returned to Glasgow to the chair of Civil Engineering in 1889; and Andrew Gray succeeded Kelvin in the chair of Natural Philosophy in 1899. Better laboratory teaching required new buildings and, after a considerable struggle, these began to be provided; more importantly more assistants and demonstrators were employed by the University and were no longer paid out of the professor's own pocket. With the recent availability of research grants, particularly from the Carnegie Trust, it was also possible to develop postgraduate teaching which until

Top: Professor Bower and his staff in Botany in about 1900.
Bottom: Lord Kelvin with his marine compass.

then had been available only in Cambridge and London and in German universities. At the beginning of the century these pioneers were joined by a succession of eminent scientists with a commitment to laboratory teaching. In 1902 Sir John Graham Kerr, a Cambridge evolutionary embryologist, became professor of Zoology and in 1904 John Gregory, already an FRS and an outstanding researcher, was appointed to the new chair of Geology. Although the professor of Chemistry, John 'Soda' Ferguson, devoted his time to an antiquarian interest in the subject, the appointment of Frederick Soddy to the newly created lectureship in physical chemistry in 1904 brought to Glasgow a scientist at the cutting edge of investigation into radiation. In 1906 Noel Paton succeeded to the chair of Physiology and took Glasgow into the path-breaking area of research into the relationship between human diet and health, using the City's slums to test his hypotheses. All these men trained a remarkable group of young men and women who went on to make outstanding contributions in research, teaching and industry in many parts of the world.

In Medicine Sir William Macewen, a student of Lister and professor of Surgery from 1892 to 1924, strove to achieve perfect aseptic conditions in his operating theatre and excellent post-operative nursing, allowing him to pioneer some of the most advanced surgical procedures of the time including the excision of brain tumours and osteotomies for the treatment of rickets endemic in the slums of Glasgow. He was accused of failing to found a research school because of his brusque independent manner, but many of his students became celebrated surgeons. There were

Sir Henry Jones, professor of Moral Philosophy.

also advances in other areas of Medicine; Midwifery and Obstetrics with the appointments of Murdoch Cameron (1894) and Munro Kerr (1911), Materia Medica with Ralph Stockman (1897), and Forensic Medicine with John Glaister (1898).

Glasgow's transition into a modern research and teaching university was given impetus by the appointment of Sir Donald MacAlister as Principal in 1907. A pre-eminent medical administrator, he perceived clearly the need to recruit staff who would use research to inform teaching; he encouraged contact with other universities in the United Kingdom and overseas; and he was keen to extend the range of subjects in the University. He helped to establish the Muirhead and St Mungo chairs

at the Royal Infirmary in 1911 and raised endowments for chairs in Scottish History and Literature, French, German, Bacteriology, Organic Chemistry, Biochemistry, Applied Physics, Electrical Engineering, Mechanical Engineering, Public Health, Child Health, Italian, Spanish, Accountancy and Music and succeeded in attracting able researchers to many of them. E P Cathcart, the first Gardiner professor of Biochemistry and later professor of Physiology, a gifted experimental physiologist, built up a loyal and dedicated research team building on the work started by Noel Paton. Leonard Findlay, the first Samson Gemmell professor of Child Health, was the first paediatrician to use biochemical techniques in the investigation and diagnosis of diseases in infants and pioneered new techniques in the treatment of rickets, rheumatic fever and congenital

The Natural Philosophy laboratory in about 1900.

syphilis. Sir Robert Muir, professor of Pathology (1899–1936), created an outstanding department from which it is said most of the chairs in the United Kingdom were at one time filled. William Entwistle, the first professor of Spanish, after a distinguished career at Glasgow where he examined the influence of the Arthurian legend on Spanish literature, went on to become professor of Spanish Studies in Oxford.

Expansion on this scale demanded more space for laboratories and the library; but the new building programme of the early 1920s was brought to a halt by the long inter-war depression from which the West of Scotland's traditional industries never fully recovered. It was impossible for MacAlister's successors

97

to follow his example by raising endowments locally for either new posts or buildings. Moreover Glasgow lacked the new industries in sectors such as food processing and pharmaceuticals that were willing to sponsor applied research in universities south of the border. Most seriously the severity of the depression and accompanying unemployment coupled with the actions of 'Red Clydeside' activists during the war gained Glasgow an unwarranted reputation as a city of gang violence and appalling slums. This made it harder to attract both good staff and research students from further afield.

By the time Sir Hector Hetherington returned as Principal in 1936, the University was in some difficulty. Declining undergrad-

uate numbers were straining the finances at a time when science, engineering and medicine urgently required more space and equipment to keep abreast of new developments. Geology under Battersby Bailey still maintained its reputation as an outstanding centre of research. Natural Philosophy under the good-natured Professor Taylor Jones had lost direction and although Chemistry had a new Institute building, it lacked intellectual leadership. Edward Hindle, who had just succeeded to the chair of Zoology, was more interested in re-organising the curriculum and the OTC than in directing research at which he was very skilled. All the medical departments were suffering because of the acute financial problems of both the voluntary and public hospitals, exacerbated by the need to buy the latest x-ray equipment vital for diagnostic and clinical research. In the humanities, with important exceptions, there was little to inspire. Hetherington was

Professor Ian Donald scanning his unborn grandchild, 1980.

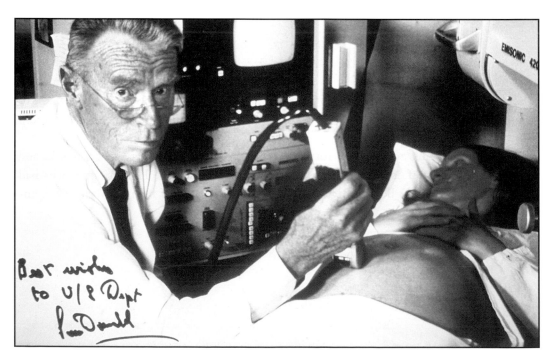

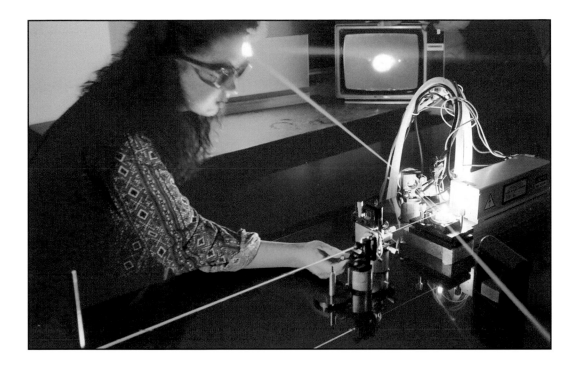

Laser research laboratory, 1993.

determined at least to foster the established areas of research excellence in science and medicine by recruiting the best staff he could get and at the same time developing long-term plans for new facilities. In 1939 he made a start with the appointment of the exceptionally gifted young surgeon, Charles Illingworth, to the chair of Surgery.

Despite the hiatus caused by the war, Hetherington kept his eyes on the future, planning to allow staff in all but Arts to divide their time equally between teaching and research as soon after the war as possible. In 1940 Sir James W Cook, a leading researcher into carcinogenic chemicals, was appointed to the chair of Chemistry and two years later the brilliant crystallographer J Monteath Robertson was recruited to the Gardiner chair of Organic Chemistry. In 1943 Philip Dee, then leading one of the

path-breaking radar research teams, was appointed professor of Natural Philosophy but did not take up the post until after the war. C M Yonge, a distinguished marine biologist, came to the chair of Zoology in 1944. These appointments were designed to encourage a research culture which would attract funding from new government agencies such as the Department of Scientific and Industrial Research. Hetherington, who had been a member of many government committees concerning social policy, realised that changes in the health services and medical education were inevitable. From 1945 he began to make full-time professorial clinical appointments in the expectation that the holders would have greater freedom to teach, practice their specialities and carry out research. The concentration of medical education in the University in 1947 (page 110), the creation of the National Health Service (NHS) in 1948, and the post-war revitalisation of the Faculty of Physicians and Surgeons of Glasgow (the Royal College of Physicians and Surgeons from 1962) as a centre for postgraduate medical education all contributed to the University's commitment to research and continuing professional training.

In the 1950s the priority was to secure funds for new buildings and perhaps more importantly for expensive experimental equipment needed to sustain leading-edge research in engineering and science. A vital part of this strategy was Dee's determination to promote research on the nuclear sciences through the installation of a 330 MeV electron synchrotron. Eventually commissioned in 1954, over the next decade it was used to carry out a programme of experiments which made Glasgow once more an international centre for physical research. Fundamental to research across the sciences and engineering was the acquisition of one of the new computers for intensive numerical processing. Permission was given in 1955; but it was another four years before the first computer was inaugurated. Lack of support from local industry meant that it was too small to be a very useful research tool and it was not until 1964 that Glasgow acquired a powerful mainframe. During the 1950s engineering was also reinvigorated by the appointment of a number of men with extensive research experience gained in wartime, particularly G D S MacLellan to the Rankine chair of Mechanics and Engineering and John Lamb to the chair of Electrical Engineering. Testimony to the revitalisation

of research in science and engineering in the immediate post war years was the rapid growth in the number of research students, with Ph.D.s awarded in science subjects reaching a new peak of 78 in 1962–3.

The benefits of full-time professorial appointments to the clinical departments quickly became evident. The use of radio-active isotopes in the investigation and treatment of thyroid and related problems heralded the development of nuclear medicine. The recruitment of the gifted researcher Ian Donald, who had seen radar in use during the war, to the chair of Midwifery in 1954 led to the trail-blazing development of ultra-sound imaging for the non-invasive examination of the developing human foetus and later of other organs. Cardiac surgery was initiated at Glasgow Royal Infirmary by Professor W Arthur Mackey and progressively developed from closed to open heart surgery for the treatment of congenital and acquired cardiac disease and, most recently, to cardiac transplantation. The surge of medical progress led to a considerable increase in the number of chairs, particularly in the developing areas of medicine – since 1959 in Anaesthetics, Dermatology, Neurology, Neurosurgery, Pathological Biochemistry, Medical Cardiology, Cardiac Surgery, Medical Genetics, Geriatric Medicine, Medical Oncology, Radiation Oncology, Child and Adolescent Psychiatry, General Practice, and more recently in Rheumatology, Human Nutrition, and Paediatric Medicine. All these clinical developments took place in general harmony with the rapidly expanding NHS. The clinical services given to the NHS by full-time professors and their staff were broadly balanced by the invaluable contribution of NHS staff to clinical teaching, many of whom carried out important research and made substantial contributions to the development of their subjects.

Although the emphasis was on scientific and medical research, the University did not entirely neglect the humanities, particularly the fast-developing area of social science. There were successes, particularly in economics. Sir Alec Cairncross was enticed back as professor of Applied Economics in 1950 and at once embarked on an ambitious programme of research. When he left for the Treasury in 1961, he was succeeded by the talented Donald Robertson. Sydney Checkland came to the new chair of Economic History in 1957 and began to develop a research centre built around the study of Glasgow's great nineteenth-century industrial and commercial enterprises. The following year Tom Wilson, an Oxford economist, succeeded to the chair of Political Economy, bringing a theoretical Keynesian perspective to the discipline. There were distinguished scholars in Politics; David Daiches Raphael, later Director of Imperial College, was the first Edward Caird professor, and Bill Mackenzie, a noted constitutionalist, the first professor of government.

In the humanities the research culture was much slower to develop, partly because Hetherington did not believe that it was necessary and partly because the teaching load remained very heavy. There were distinguished scholars in Arts but there were very few postgraduate students. Most able graduates were encouraged to go elsewhere, particularly to Oxford, Cambridge and

London. It was not until the massive expansion in staff numbers in the mid-1960s that postgraduate numbers increased and even then the number of Ph.D.s awarded in humanities and social science did not exceed twenty until 1978.

During the 1970s and 1980s new areas of research in the sciences, engineering and medicine were built on the strong foundations already laid. For example Naval Architecture, which lost the traditional market for its expertise because of the collapse of Clyde shipbuilding, diversified into research into semi-submersible structures used in the developing North Sea oil industry. Important advances continued to be made in diagnostic and therapeutic techniques in collaboration with researchers in the life sciences, transformed by the advent of molecular biology. The creation of an experimental condensed matter group in Physics in 1973 gave Glasgow a world lead in micromagnetic structural studies. Buildings were constructed to support emerging areas of research, such as Botany at Garscube and the Genetics and Virology buildings at Gilmorehill. In some areas there was change in emphasis towards national if not international facilities as 'big' science became increasingly more expensive. For example the successor to the synchrotron was the European international laboratory CERN at Geneva where Glasgow physicists were involved from the 1960s and in the 1980s made a major contribution to the research programme. The most powerful computational facilities were available only at certain sites and individual departments had to concentrate their expertise on select areas of research. This had the effect of encouraging closer links between institutions and between different disciplines within the university, bringing greater cohesiveness and sense of common purpose.

Success hastened Glasgow to have one of the largest spreads of research activity of any university in the United Kingdom. By the mid-1990s the University is winning over £44 million a year in research grants and contracts, with a further £21 million coming from the Government in basic research support.

Top: Business Record Centre.
Bottom: Ocean Engineering wavetank.

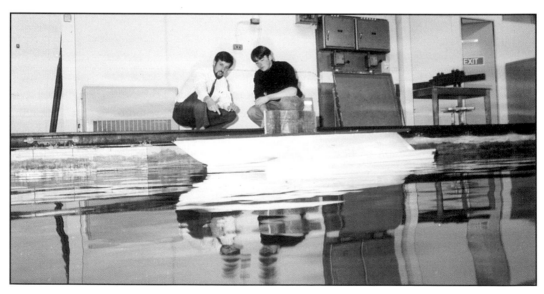

CHAPTER 7

Governing Gilmorehill

The 1870 building on Gilmorehill reflected the administrative structure of the time. There was an imposing Senate Room, grand accommodation for the Clerk of Senate and a small Court Room tucked away under the stairs to the Museum. There was no Bursar's office because the finances of the University, in the hands of factors since 1577, were now managed by a firm of Glasgow lawyers with offices in the city centre. The Secretary of the University Court was a practising lawyer in town. The only permanent members of the administration on Gilmorehill were the Assistant Secretary of Court and the Registrar and the two posts were later combined. It was soon recognised that the 1858 Act had given too much power to the Senate and too little to the newly established University Court, successor of the old Faculty (page 28), and a further Royal Commission on Scottish Universities, set up in 1876, recommended that their functions and membership should be better balanced. The Universities (Scotland) Act of 1889 therefore vested all university property and control of all finances in the Court. In Glasgow its membership was extended to four representatives each of the Senate and the General Council, with the community represented by the Lord Provost of Glasgow and an assessor of the Lord Provost, Magistrates and Council. It continued to be chaired by the Rector; the Principal, the Chancellor's assessor and the Rector's assessor retained their places; but the Dean of Faculties was omitted. The Court also became directly responsible for all appointments in its patronage and could nominate up to a third of the membership of the committees responsible for managing the University Library and the Hunterian Museum. The Senate remained responsible for all academic matters. The only person who had a permanent place on both bodies was the Principal, now the dynamic and progressive John Caird, whose power and role were not defined. The Act made professors salaried and no longer dependent for their income on class fees, which were now to be collected by the University. This placed a heavy burden on the University as the fee income was insufficient to met the new salary bills. In an effort to ensure uniformity of practice and in lip-service to the idea of a national university, the Act also required that any Ordinance made by a Scottish university should be approved by the Senates and General Councils of the other three universities before ratification by the Privy Council.

The 1889 Act extended for a further nine years the powers of the Commissioners appointed originally under the 1858 Act to carry through reforms. They oversaw the widening and improvement of the curriculum envisaged by the Royal Commission, notably through the introduction of new subjects and honours teaching, the reorganisation of science degrees and the creation of science faculties (pages 85–6). Recognising that universities lacked the funds to achieve these reforms, the Commissioners secured an annual Treasury grant for Glasgow of just over £12,000 but from the outset this was completely inadequate to support the changes, the new chairs, the stipends of the less well-paid professors and the pensions of those who had retired. And in 1897 the cost of pensions increased when the Commissioners at last made it possible for professors to retire on grounds other than ill-health. The Commissioners had further powers with financial implications, in particular to admit women students on equal terms with men and authorise amalgamations with affiliated colleges. In Glasgow this led to the merger with Queen Margaret College in 1892 and the acquisition of its large endowments which helped relieve the hard-pressed finances (page 35).

The West End Park with Trinity College towers in the background, 1901.

Sir Donald MacAlister leading representatives of the Russian Duma on their visit to Glasgow in 1911.

And in 1899 the Commissioners encouraged the University to come to an understanding with the newly formed West of Scotland Agricultural College to offer a joint course leading to a B.Sc. degree in Agriculture.

One consequence of the 1889 reforms, perhaps unforeseen, was the growth in authority of the Principal, who ceased to be the first amongst equals and became in effect an academic administrator with the authority to determine the future direction of the University. From 1889 to 1929 Glasgow was fortunate to have three Principals of exceptional vision, who were determined to expand facilities and explore new territory. John Caird (1873–98) and Robert Story (1898–1907) had begun their careers as parish ministers in the Church of Scotland, albeit with experience of Church governance and theological debate. Both held a wide view of the role of the University in society and neither regarded the scientific revolution as a threat to their own beliefs. Caird, committed to a social vision of the Christian gospels, advocated extra-mural education and the higher education of women; and Story, who looked more like a patriarch than a man of affairs, used the ninth jubilee in 1901 as a platform to raise funds for the new buildings essential for modern science teaching. Sir Donald MacAlister (1907–29) had already achieved distinction as President of the General Medical Council, a position he continued to hold until 1931. He believed firmly in the importance of such national organisations. He supported the Home

Universities Committee and in 1911 helped to establish and then chaired the Universities' Bureau of the Empire (later the Association of Commonwealth Universities) and the Committee of Vice-Chancellors and Principals. After the formation in 1919 of the University Grants Committee (UGC) as the vehicle for distributing government funds, the CVCP and its chairman were crucial in making the needs of the universities known.

One of MacAlister's first pre-occupations was to come to an understanding with the Glasgow and West of Scotland Technical College, founded in 1887 by the merger of a number of existing institutions including the Mechanics' Institute and the major part of the Andersonian Institution. A Court committee appointed to review relations with the College in 1906 took two years to report and MacAlister, dissatisfied with the slow progress, personally took charge of the complex negotiations, concluded only in May 1911 and sanctioned by the Privy Council in 1913. The College had become the Royal Technical College in 1912 and under the terms of an affiliation ordinance students of the RTC could matriculate in the University and receive Glasgow degrees in Applied Science, including engineering, applied chemistry, architecture, and pharmacy. Joint Boards of Studies and examiners were established and the Chemistry departments of the two institutions began to work closely together. Sadly no sooner had he concluded this agreement than MacAlister became desperately ill and was never free from pain for the rest of his life. He happened to be convalescing in Germany on the declaration of hostilities in 1914 and was briefly detained as a prisoner

of war, but returned to lead the University with the help of the Factors and Dr David Murray, Chairman of the Finance Committee, almost unscathed through the immense difficulties of the war years. With great foresight and courage he began raising money during and immediately after the war was able to endow lectureships and chairs in new disciplines such as Medical Radiology and Russian – both dear to his heart. Between 1919 and his retirement ten years later he raised endowments for no less than fifteen chairs and several lectureships, and funds for many building projects including the University Chapel and the Arts building in the West Quadrangle. Following another Universities (Scotland) Act in 1922, which

Principal Story.

he had helped draft, he pushed through Ordinances widening membership of Senate to include nominated readers and lecturers and introduced a pension scheme for all academic staff with a retiring age of 65 – although 70 in the case of the Principal. Astonishingly he achieved all this without so much as the help of a secretary, writing all his letters himself and personally taking minutes of meetings. He expected all professors to follow his example and refused to allow the appointment of secretaries. By the end of his career, unable to climb the stairs to the University Offices without pain, he conducted business from the Lodgings, employing a young graduate Robert Hutcheson (later to be the Secretary of Court) as a runner to carry his instructions. The only change he did not whole-

heartedly support was the creation of a separate Faculty of Engineering in 1923, the brainchild of the professor of Civil Engineering, John Dewar Cormack.

In 1929 MacAlister retired and was succeeded by the popular Sir Robert Sangster Rait, the Professor of Scottish History and Literature. This was the year the Church of Scotland was reunited with the United Free Church of Scotland, itself an amalgamation of various secession churches in 1901. Re-union caused massive upheaval as both Churches had congregations in most parishes in Scotland. Many congregations amalgamated and many churches were closed. It was no longer necessary to retain separate colleges for training Free Church clergy and in 1935 the United Free Church College, established in Glasgow as Trinity College in 1856, merged with the University's Faculty of Divinity.

The Duke and Duchess of York with Principal Rait on the right and the Rector, 1936.

The College had a distinguished history with some leading scholars as professors and it had trained many clergy who served throughout the United Kingdom and overseas, particularly in North America, India and Dominion countries. Its imposing classical building, designed by Charles Wilson and dominated by three towers, opposite the University on the Park Hill, was used by the Divinity Faculty until its sale for conversion to housing in the 1980s but the College with its own endowments continues to be part of the University.

Professors in many disciplines were still in charge of only small departments but in the interwar years more secure financing from the UGC allowed more junior staff to be appointed, though on what now seem hard terms. There were two grades: lecturers with five-year renewable contracts and assistants

(not assistant lecturers) and demonstrators whose contracts were renewable annually for a maximum of three years. Despite the growth in numbers, the ratio of staff to students was much lower than in universities south of the border. The professor remained an autocratic, often remote figure, who determined the syllabus and shouldered the burden of much of the Ordinary class lecturing. Lecturers were there largely to assist the professor in the formidable task of marking essays, assignments and examinations, and to teach more advanced classes. Remarkably in an effort to appear less Olympian than his predecessor, Rait refused to use the Principal's office on the first floor of the South Front; and instead moved to a small room on the ground floor. Sadly, Rait, with first-hand

Students welcoming Principal Hetherington at Glasgow Central Station, 1936.

Rhona Mackie, Professor of Dermatology, in 1993.

knowledge of the effect of the economic slump in his own family business, was depressed and ill and failed to provide leadership during five critical years.

The appointment of Sir Hector Hetherington as Principal in 1936 brought back to Glasgow one of the most able university administrators of his generation, who MacAlister, years earlier, had marked out as his successor. With nine years of experience as Vice Chancellor at the University of Liverpool, Hetherington knew that plans must be prepared urgently for better research facilities and rising student numbers as soon as the effects of the depression were past. He encouraged the professors to think hard about the future and even authorised the appointment of departmental secretaries to give them time to do so. The well-developed expansion scheme worked out over the next three years was interrupted by the war; but

as the prospect of victory grew nearer, the government began to plan for the post-war universities. A series of national committees reviewed medical, dental and veterinary training and recommended that all existing independent schools should be amalgamated with universities. As a result in 1945 the Glasgow Veterinary College, founded in 1862, became a sub-faculty of the University's Medical Faculty and later a faculty in its own right, with the gifted William Weipers as first Director of Veterinary Education. In 1947 the two independent colleges of medicine in Glasgow – Anderson's College of Medicine (page 48) and St Mungo's College (page 22) became part of the University's Medical Faculty and their buildings were used to house University medical departments. The Glasgow Dental School, established in 1879 as part of the Andersonian Institution with premises in the Dental Hospital in Renfrew Street and independent since 1887, also became part of the Medical Faculty but continued to be based in the Dental Hospital. Implicit in these mergers was an expansion of vocational opportunities in all three professions and an increase in student places, placing a considerable burden on the administration of the university. This was more than compensated, however, by the increase in consultant posts following the creation of the NHS, with a greatly enlarged pool of clinical teachers and researchers.

Towards the end of the war, the role of the UGC was expanded to include the finance of new building and other capital projects, and the possibility of expansion became much more certain. With funding on the scale now envisaged and the growing numbers of staff and students, it was no longer practical for the University to have a part-time Secretary of Court or employ factors to handle its finances. In 1944 Sir John Spencer Muirhead resigned as Secretary of Court and was succeeded as first full-time Secretary by Dr Robert Hutcheson, the Registrar, and in the following year a Finance Office was established at Gilmorehill. Assistant Secretaries of Court were appointed to handle functions such as staff appointments; the post of Assistant Registrar was revived; faculty clerks and additional advisers of studies were appointed; and a Works Department created to supervise the massive post-war building programme.

Throughout the 1950s the University attempted to redefine its relationship with the Royal Technical College, which because of its association with Glasgow had always been recognised by the UGC as having university status. The affiliation ordinance of 1913 had become a source of friction almost

immediately after it was signed and matters came to a head when the government called for an expansion in technical and engineering education. The choice was either greater autonomy for the RTC or closer co-operation. There was a long, heated and often bitter debate and eventually as a short-term expedient a revised ordinance was approved in 1957. By then the College had changed its name to the Royal College of Science and Technology and in 1964 it became the core component of a second university in the City, the new University of Strathclyde.

In 1963 the Robbins Committee recommended a large-scale expansion of higher education throughout the United Kingdom and dual support for teaching and research in all disciplines. Some of its proposals required legislation in a further Universities (Scotland) Act in 1966, amongst them the abolition of the requirement for new ordinances to be approved by the General Councils and Senates of other institutions, a reform which allowed Glasgow immediately to make curricula more flexible. One important consequence of the Government's acceptance of Robbins was a very large increase in the number of both students and staff and most staff came to hold tenured posts. The growth in staff numbers and the recognition of dual funding for research and teaching was of particular benefit to the Arts. Relations between humanities and the rapidly expanding social sciences became strained and in 1977 a separate Social Sciences faculty embracing economics, economic history, politics, sociology, social administration and psychology was created.

Although Glasgow was slow to respond to

demands from both junior staff and students for representation on governing bodies and for more open governance, it did not, as in many other universities in Britain and Europe, make a common cause to bring about change by public protest. It was not until the late 1960s that steps were taken to modernise the management structure and then only after long exchanges. From the late 1970s heads of department, no longer necessarily professors, were to be nominated after a period of consultation. There were to be regular departmental meetings, reducing the authority of the professors, and elected non-professorial and later ancilliary staff and students became members of Court.

Rapid expansion came to an abrupt halt in 1974 with a reduction in government grants at a time when inflation was over twenty per cent. The crisis was so serious that the Principal Sir Charles Wilson began to write regular letters to all staff outlining the University's plans. Much more savage pruning of university funding followed during the 1980s. Although Glasgow escaped relatively lightly in comparison with some universities, the number of UGC-funded staff fell, forcing the University to make good the shortfall from the private sector, notably educational charities and industry. This policy heralded a sea-change in academic management. Professors and heads of department had now to be not only able teachers and scholars, but also entrepreneurs – good at raising money. At the same time government was seeking to widen access to higher education without making additional funds available. In 1984 the Scottish Tertiary Education Advisory Council (STEAC) was established to review

provision for tertiary education, with Sir Alwyn Williams, now the Principal of the University, as the only university member. STEAC reported in 1985 and recommended the creation of a separate Scottish funding council for higher education, something the University had strongly opposed in the 1970s. The Scottish Higher Education Funding Council (SHEFC) was created in 1993 and as STEAC envisaged, SHEFC is committed to protecting the unique features of the Scottish system of university education, particularly the four-year Honours degree.

Simultaneously the government as part of wider policies was calling for more account-ability by universities for their teaching and research. This was to be achieved by imple-menting the findings of the Committee of Vice Chancellors and Principals (CVCP) Steering Committee for Efficiency Studies in Universities, which proposed a radical overhaul of management structures and greater use of performance indicators. At Glasgow this resulted in the formation of a formal Management Group, chaired by the Principal, with day-to-day responsibility for administration, and the formation of a number of Planning Units composed of cognate academic and administrative departments. Since their inception these new structures have been required to meet an avalanche of demands from funding bodies; ranging from responses to research selectivity exercises, to teaching-quality assessment, and to open competition for funds for research and inno-vation in learning. They have also had to cope with further reductions in government funding and in the case of the Medical Faculty, with the reorganisation of the NHS.

The Universities of Glasgow and Strathclyde collaborate on a database of equine information.

Glasgow has done well in meeting these challenges by winning more and more of its income from other sources.

In broad outline the structure of the University has remained relatively unaltered since 1889. The Court continues to be responsible for finance, appointments and property and to direct the increasingly complex administration. The Senate continues to control academic affairs but the enormous increase in the number of professors led to the creation of a College of Senators in 1996, with the full Senate meeting less frequently. Since the move to Gilmorehill, Glasgow has been fortunate in attracting many laymen of distinction to serve as assessors on its Court, and give freely of their time and experience. These have included Sir William Lorimer, the celebrated Scottish architect, Sir William Robieson, formerly the editor of the *Glasgow Herald*, and in recent times Sir Robert Smith, a distinguished Scottish accountant and man of business. The duties of the Principal have also grown dramatically as the size of the University has increased. The first two vice-principals were appointed in 1972 for a fixed term and by the late 1980s there were four. In modern times Glasgow has had chancellors – elected by the graduates – who have taken a keen interest in the University's fortunes, regularly attending meetings of the General Council and presiding over annual honorary graduations. These have included Lord Kelvin (1904–8), Sir Donald MacAlister (1929–34), Sir Daniel Macaulay Stevenson (1934–46), one of the University's greatest benefactors, Lord Boyd-Orr (1946–72) and Sir Alec Cairncross (1972–96).

For all the changes in its perception and functions, the governance of the modern University has been remarkably consistent, in part certainly because of the compact campus established on Gilmorehill in 1870.

113

University museum display.

CHAPTER 8

Towards 2001

by the Principal, Sir Graeme Davies

The last decade of the century, as the eleventh jubilee approaches in 2001, is as challenging as any period in the history of the University. There was substantial expansion in student numbers in the early 1990s encouraged by the Universities Funding Council. This placed severe pressure on accommodation for teaching and research and an ambitious series of new building and refurbishment projects were put in place by the then Principal, Sir William Kerr Fraser (1988–95). They have left the University well positioned to meet the subsequent government policy of consolidation of student numbers in the latter half of the decade. Consolidation however applied only to undergraduate numbers and this has encouraged an expansion of postgraduate programmes of both taught courses and research. These will be a high priority in the years ahead, building upon the breadth and depth of scholarly and research expertise which exists within the academic staff.

A range of services has been created to improve teaching and learning. Staff development and teaching enhancement have been guided by the work of the Teaching and Learning Service. And self-learning for students has been encouraged by the widespread involvement of staff in aspects of the Teaching and Learning Technology Programme sponsored by the Funding Councils. This has been complemented by the University's national responsibility for two centres within the Computers in Teaching Initiative – in History with Archaeology and Art History and in Statistics. Departments with the support of the University's Quality Assurance Office have achieved a high level of success in the Scottish Higher Education Funding Council (SHEFC) quality assessment programme. The University has also continued its outreach programmes designed to bring students with non-traditional entrance qualifications and from deprived areas of Glasgow and the region into higher education. And there is a growing number of continuing professional development and adult liberal education courses in Adult and Continuing Education and a commitment to further development of distance learning programmes.

In research there has been a positive response to the increasing pressure on resources caused by a substantial 'squeeze' on public funding – by active management of programmes directed at strengthening the basic and strategic research capabilities of the University as well as preparing for the 1996 Research Assessment Exercise conducted by the Funding Councils. There has been notable success in gaining support from outside agencies such as the Research Councils, the Wellcome Trust and the Leukaemia Research Fund, and a number of individual awards in excess of £1 million have been won. The University has had a long-term commitment to collaborative research with business and industry in a wide range of disciplines and activities. In 1993 more than 20 per cent of its research income came from this source and that income is growing. Industrial income has grown from £15.7m and 206 contracts in 1991–2 to £20.1m and 339 contracts in 1994–5. Glasgow has consistently been in the top five of UK universities for its income from industry world-wide – 20 per cent coming from Scotland; 55 per cent from the rest of the UK; 15 per cent from Europe; and 10 per cent from the rest of the world.

Universities have recently become much more evidently part of national economic development. They are much more commercially aware and they have much to offer. For example Glasgow University plays an

important role in technology transfer. In 1994–5 it earned some £375,000 through twenty licensing agreements and currently holds 105 patents in whole or in part. It is also part of a round dozen joint venture companies. Targeting Technology Limited established with the Glasgow Development Agency (GDA) and Strathclyde University seeks to ensure the optimal success of technology in small firms. And another joint venture, Services to Software Limited, with Glasgow Caledonian University, the National Engineering Laboratory at East Kilbride and the GDA has been established to assist smaller software-based companies, particularly the 200–300 small and medium-sized enterprises in Scotland, by providing business support and advice on how to access software expertise within the Universities.

Universities produce an essential national commodity – graduates – and a high proportion of Glasgow graduates take up employment in business and industry and the professions, many in Scotland. There is now a system of mass higher education in the UK and the Government has recognised the need to reassure employers that the expansion of higher education has not been at the expense of quality. The Secretary of State has therefore introduced both quality audit and quality assessment of teaching and learning and Glasgow now directs much effort to evaluating the quality of teaching, the subjects, their content and the way they are presented and examined.

Course innovation to meet the needs of the industry and business is an important part of the University's work. For example Product

Design Engineering is a recent collaborative programme with the Glasgow School of Art that balances the technical, creative, ergonomic and psychological aspects of the design process. Innovations such as these are complemented by a range of professional development courses, for example the new Forensic Engineering programme which seeks to evaluate, analyse, investigate and report on failures to meet design objectives. And innovation is not restricted to the technologies. Seminars have been set up for senior managers in the tourist industry involved in formulating strategy and covering customer-focused quality, effective marketing of visitor attractions and heritage briefings. There is a new MBA programme sponsored by the Lanarkshire Development Agency involving nineteen companies in the region. The University is also investigating and developing 'home and campus' studies combining distance learning and conventional education on the campus. And there is the potential for further development of courses in the workplace.

Universities also make financial, social, cultural, professional, environmental and physical contributions to the communities of which they are part. Glasgow University is a major business and a major employer. With a staff of 5,300 it is among the largest employers in the city. With an income in 1994–5 of just over £189 million it is fifteenth in Metropolitan Glasgow's Top 200 enterprises.

The University has also a major social and cultural role in the life of the City. The value of some of the public amenities it provides, for example the Hunterian Museum and the Hunterian Art Gallery, is self-evident. But its

Sir Graeme Davies

contacts with the community go much, much wider. There is an extensive number of public lectures, many given by eminent visitors. There are concerts, exhibitions, open days and tours. And recently the University began to publish a regular 'notice board' circular 'Prospect' which is sent to 27,500 homes in the vicinity of the University. Our Visitors Centre, which recently won a national award, is close to University Avenue and provides a welcoming base for visitors, offering information about the University and what can be seen in the precinct. And this year has seen the beginning of the refurbishment of the Gilmorehill Halls, facing the Glasgow University Union, as a state-of-the-art Department of Theatre, Film and Television Studies with a theatre and cinema open to the public.

The earlier chapters of this short history tell of the University's distinguished past. Its vigour, its richness of expertise and its commitment to excellence must surely give it an equally distinguished future.

Statistical table

NUMBERS OF GLASGOW UNIVERSITY MATRICULATED STUDENTS.

YEAR	MEN	WOMEN	TOTAL	YEAR	MEN	WOMEN	TOTAL
1870–71	1,279	0	1,279	1933–34	3,888	1,338	5,226
1871–72	1,349	0	1,349	1934–35	3,880	1,176	5,056
1872–73	1,258	0	1,258	1935–36	3,865	1,084	4,949
1873–74	1,333	0	1,333	1936–37	3,821	1,015	4,836
1874–75	1,484	0	1,484	1937–38	3,737	1,033	4,770
1875–76	1,601	0	1,601	1938–39	3,668	1,103	4,771
1876–77	1,773	0	1,773	1939–40	3,115	1,183	4,298
1877–78	2,018	0	2,018	1940–41	2,692	1,234	3,926
1878–79	2,096	0	2,096	1941–42	2,613	1,273	3,886
1879–80	2,235	0	2,235	1942–43	2,379	1,354	3,733
1880–81	2,304	0	2,304	1943–44	2,206	1,330	3,536
1881–82	2,320	0	2,320	1944–45	2,220	1,342	3,562
1882–83	2,275	0	2,275	1945–46	2,833	1,407	4,240
1883–84	2,212	0	2,212	1946–47	4,262	1,426	5,688
1884–85	2,261	0	2,261	1947–48	5,594	1,487	7,081
1885–86	2,241	0	2,241	1948–49	6,044	1,452	7,496
1886–87	2,260	0	2,260	1949–50	5,922	1,461	7,383
1887–88	2,188	0	2,188	1950–51	5,656	1,411	7,067
1888–89	2,104	0	2,104	1951–52	5,225	1,352	6,577
1889–90	2,180	0	2,180	1952–53	4,872	1,320	6,192
1890–91	2,166	0	2,166	1953–54	4,770	1,277	6,047
1891–92	2,138	0	2,138	1954–55	4,732	1,294	6,026
1892–93	2,049	131	2,180	1955–56	4,796	1,391	6,187
1893–94	1,915	165	2,080	1956–57	4,923	1,429	6,352
1894–95	1,695	208	1,903	1957–58	5,117	1,487	6,604
1895–96	1,629	246	1,875	1958–59	5,356	1,526	6,882
1896–97	1,676	248	1,924	1959–60	5,492	1,581	7,073
1897–98	1,563	257	1,820	1960–61	5,429	1,646	7,075
1898–99	1,647	306	1,953	1961–62	5,293	1,767	7,060
1899–1900	1,694	343	2,037	1962–63	5,587	1,934	7,521
1900–01	1,692	341	2,033	1963–64	5,706	2,001	7,707
1901–02	1,699	360	2,059	1964–65	5,642	2,071	7,713
1902–03	1,797	344	2,141	1965–66	5,749	2,185	7,934
1903–04	1,807	395	2,202	1966–67	5,630	2,341	7,971
1904–05	1,855	417	2,272	1967–68	5,952	2,543	8,495
1905–06	1,881	512	2,393	1968–69	6,222	2,659	8,881
1906–07	1,918	586	2,504	1969–70	6,306	2,796	9,102
1907–08	1,905	589	2,494	1970–71	6,247	3,020	9,267
1908–09	2,004	695	2,699	1971–72	6,208	3,200	9,408
1909–10	2,086	642	2,728	1972–73	6,067	3,406	9,473
1910–11	2,108	682	2,790	1973–74	6,101	3,590	9,691
1911–12	2,113	681	2,794	1974–75	6,203	3,803	10,006
1912–13	2,187	648	2,835	1975–76	6,166	4,079	10,245
1913–14	2,254	662	2,916	1976–77	6,327	4,256	10,583
1914–15	1,835	635	2,470	1977–78	6,357	4,221	10,578
1915–16	1,164	658	1,822	1978–79	6,290	4,272	10,562
1916–17	909	753	1,662	1979–80	6,460	4,528	10,988
1917–18	1,049	872	1,921	1980–81	6,411	4,630	11,041
1918–19	2,113	955	3,068	1981–82	6,473	5,109	11,582
1919–20	3,177	1,027	4,204	1982–83	6,507	5,297	11,804
1920–21	3,585	1,142	4,727	1983–84	6,781	5,366	12,147
1921–22	3,635	1,221	4,856	1984–85	6,961	5,401	12,362
1922–23	3,543	1,353	4,896	1985–86	7,242	5,778	13,020
1923–24	3,275	1,419	4,694	1986–87	7,272	5,754	13,026
1924–25	3,069	1,529	4,598	1987–88	6,914	5,180	12,094
1925–26	3,049	1,440	4,489	1988–89	6,958	5,409	12,367
1926–27	3,292	1,489	4,781	1989–90	7,170	5,793	12,963
1927–28	3,624	1,670	5,294	1990–91	7,530	6,282	13,812
1928–29	3,803	1,693	5,496	1991–92	7,584	6,498	14,082
1929–30	3,845	1,682	5,527	1992–93	8,087	7,302	15,389
1930–31	3,898	1,633	5,531	1993–94	8,686	7,978	16,664
1931–32	3,989	1,591	5,580	1994–95	8,358	8,477	16,835
1932–33	3,986	1,527	5,513	1995–96	8,574	9,105	17,679

Footnote: The figures up to 1986-87 include numbers of matriculated students at the Associated Colleges.

Index